Psalms

Other SkyLight Paths Books
by M. Basil Pennington, OCSO

The Song of Songs: A Spiritual Commentary
   with illustrations by Phillip Ratner

The Monks of Mount Athos: A Western Monk's Extraordinary Spiritual
   Journey on Eastern Holy Ground
   (Foreword by Archimandrite Dionysios)

Finding Grace at the Center: The Beginning of Centering Prayer
   with Thomas Keating, OCSO, and Thomas E. Clarke, SJ
   (Foreword by Rev. Cynthia Bourgeault, PhD)

Psalms

A SPIRITUAL COMMENTARY

Meditations by Abbot M. Basil Pennington, ocso
Illustrations by Phillip Ratner

Walking Together, Finding the Way®
SKYLIGHT PATHS®
PUBLISHING
Woodstock, Vermont

www.skylightpaths.com

Psalms:
A Spiritual Commentary

2008 First Quality Paperback Printing
2006 First Hardcover Printing
© 2006 by the Cistercian Abbey of Spencer, Inc.

Library of Congress Cataloging-in-Publication Data

Pennington, M. Basil.
Psalms : a spiritual commentary / by M. Basil Pennington ; illustrations by Phillip Ratner.
   p. cm.
Includes bibliographical references.
ISBN-13: 978-1-59473-141-9 (hardcover)
ISBN-10: 1-59473-141-1 (hardcover)
1. Bible. O.T. Psalms—Meditations. I. Ratner, Phillip. II. Title.

BS1430.54.P47 2005
223'.2077—dc22
ISBN-13: 978-1-59473-234-8 (quality pbk.)
ISBN-10: 1-59473-234-5 (quality pbk.)

       2005024830

10 9 8 7 6 5 4 3 2 1
Manufactured in the United States of America

SkyLight Paths Publishing is creating a place where people of different spiritual traditions come together for challenge and inspiration, a place where we can help each other understand the mystery that lies at the heart of our existence.

SkyLight Paths sees both believers and seekers as a community that increasingly transcends traditional boundaries of religion and denomination—people wanting to learn from each other, *walking together, finding the way.*

Cover Design: Sara Dismukes
Interior Design: Lisa Buckley

SkyLight Paths, "Walking Together, Finding the Way" and colophon are trademarks of LongHill Partners, Inc., registered in the U.S. Patent and Trademark Office.

Published by SkyLight Paths Publishing
A Division of LongHill Partners, Inc.
Sunset Farm Offices, Route 4, P.O. Box 237
Woodstock, VT 05091
Tel: (802) 457-4000   Fax: (802) 457-4004
www.skylightpaths.com

To the Monks of the
Abbey of Our Lady of Saint Joseph

Men of the Spirit—Men of Prayer
Men with whom I have been privileged to chant the Psalms
day by day for over fifty years.
May we sing together all the days of our lives
and for all eternity.

Moments

Welcome

Have you ever been in love? I hope so. If you have, you know a simple statement of fact just doesn't do it. "Say it with flowers," a popular ad urges us. Some of us do take recourse to flowery speech. The more talented turn to poetry, weaving beautiful garlands of words. Love poetry is a beautiful and treasured part of the literary heritage of every nation. The more talented yet turn these words into music. If we turn on the radio we usually do not need to flip the dial very long before we hear someone crooning of love or disappointment in love. The Psalms are essentially love songs giving expression to the most extraordinary love affair possible: that of God with his People, a love affair that, at least on the part of God's People, has had its ups and downs. They can give meaningful and powerful voice to our own personal love affair with this amazing God, so far beyond us, yet so truly and longingly one with us.

Benedict of Nursia's sixth-century *Rule for Monasteries* (RB) may, indeed, seem in many ways to be a rather primitive document, and many of its practical or disciplinary provisions are. But even today thousands of men and women in all parts of the world still look to it as their rule of life and commit themselves to live according to it. For there is enshrined within it great spiritual wisdom.

In his *Rule*, Benedict, in fact, says relatively little about prayer, which, of course, is central to monastic and Christian life. He sets up a powerful framework of prayer that he calls the *Opus Dei*, the Work of God. Inspired by verses of the Psalms, he calls upon the monks to gather "seven times in the day" (Ps. 119:164) and once in the night (Ps. 119:62) to sing God's praises. For each of these gatherings he allots certain Psalms as the substance of the prayer service. It is precisely here that he expects the monks to learn how to pray. Paul of Tarsus has declared quite emphatically, "We do not know how to pray as we ought," adding "but the Holy Spirit prays within us" (Rom. 8:26). In the tradition it is taught that Holy Spirit inspired the authors of the Psalms; they are inspired prayers that enable the Spirit to pray within us. Hence, the wise spiritual master, Benedict, gives but one primary directive: "Let the mind be in accord with the voice" (RB 19:7). By the provisions of the holy Legislator, the whole of the Psalter, plus some repetitions—even daily repetitions—are to be sung by the monks each week. The monk, with this constant repetition, is to allow the Psalms to form his mind and his heart; indeed, he is to allow them to teach him how to pray. The Psalms are the prayer book of monks and nuns, the members of the Christian community most totally committed to prayer. The Psalms are the school of prayer and are there for all pray-ers.

Rightly so for the disciple and follower of Christ. For it is here that the young man from Nazareth, God—though he be yet truly man and like every other man in need of growing in wisdom, grace and age—learned how to pray. From the earliest age, he would have heard the Psalms chanted in the local synagogue. As a boy moving toward his bar mitzvah, he would have studied Hebrew and the Psalms and learned to chant them with the other men in the congregation. For this very special man who became a real man of prayer—spending whole nights in prayer and escaping for a long period of solitude in the desert—the Psalms were the very fabric of his life. It is not surprising that in his hour of greatest agony and dereliction, he turns to the Psalms and prays Psalm 22: "My God, my God, why have you forsaken me." This prayer well expresses his agony but turns to an expression of hope and triumph, which took possession of his soul and led to his final victorious cry: "Father, into your hands I commend my spirit. It is complete!" (Luke 23:46; John 19:30).

If the Christian can find no better school of prayer and Christian spirit than the Psalter, the Jew, also, can turn to this same school of prayer with equal confidence. Since the days of their original composition, these wondrous hymns have filled the Temple and synagogues, leading the faithful into communion with their God.

The Psalms are certainly the great, living bridge that unites the Jewish and Christian tradition and life. Here we can pray together and stand shoulder to shoulder before God, knowing to its depths our common humanity and its call to a very special relationship with the God of Abraham, Isaac, and Jacob; the God and Father of our Lord, Jesus Christ, the rabbi from Nazareth.

One of the problems we face in meditating on the Psalms and seeking to pray them is the great cultural difference that exists between us and their authors. It is not only a matter of centuries but of ethnic and theological outlook. To take an example, if we hear and understand the word "law" as we would in our contemporary civil society, how far we would be from the rich, embracing meaning it has for the inspired singer. Law, and its synonyms—Decrees, Ordinances, Precepts, etc.— speak of Torah, the Revelation, the Word of God. Once a rabbi seeking to help me understand said, "What Jesus is to you, Torah is to us: the Word of God in human form." A traditional Catholic accustomed to finding in church, in a central place, the tabernacle with a lamp burning before it, proclaiming the Real Presence, is comfortably at home in a synagogue where the ark stands above the bema illumined by a lamp. More and more in Christian churches the Scriptures are enthroned and often honored with a lamp.

It is true we struggle with fierce statements that do not make our distinction between sin and the sinner, statements that proclaim one's enemies and the enemies of God to be totally destroyed. The authors of the Psalms were very concrete, down-to-earth people and saw sin in its concrete reality in the sinner. Without any cultural excuse, even in our times we have heard similar excesses. We need to be in touch with the deep feelings that are expressed, which arise even in our own hearts, and be willing to place them before God. We must humbly realize that they are not worthy of those who have been mercifully brought into the universal reconciliation made present in our human family by the healing grace of Christ. Yes, let us fiercely berate sin and pray for its total obliteration in longing for the liberation of all sinners including ourselves. May all enemies come to be loving and loved sons and daughters of the one heavenly Father.

Christians have sometimes rejected what are called "the cursing Psalms"—those that call down imprecations upon one's enemies—the most blood-curdling of which is Psalm 137 with its final verse, "A blessing on the one who takes your little ones and dashes them against the stone." They feel such sentiments have been left behind with the proclamation of the Gospel of Love. But we need to remember that the very One who proclaimed the Gospel of Love, in proclaiming it, was quoting the Hebrew Bible, so his law of love is in no way foreign to the Jewish tradition. Moreover, he himself prayed these "cursing Psalms." Rather than rejecting them, we need to seek the guidance and inspiration of the Spirit and of the living tradition and learn how we should pray them, letting them form our minds and hearts, our lives as the People of God.

We can be in very different moods—if that is the right

word—when we read, listen to, meditate on or try to pray the Psalms. We may be looking for practical guidance, comfort or consolation, or to express our joy and gratitude. Or we may simply be open and allow the Psalms themselves to lead us into a fitting attitude before God. I would suggest that might be the best way to approach this volume.

In the Jewish tradition the Psalms are usually referred to by their first words, much as Christians refer to be Lord's Prayer as the Our Father or the Angelic Salutation as the Hail Mary. The numbering of the Psalms used here is that of the Hebrew Bible and therefore often one higher than that found in the Vulgate translations and versions dependent on it. The translation of the Psalms is essentially my own. I have frequently been asked what English-language translation of the Bible I like best. I actually prefer the Jerusalem Bible. I think Father Alexander did a good job in producing a Bible that is beautifully written and yet still very faithful to the text as it was known at the time of his work. It has been surpassed by the New Jerusalem Bible, which benefits from later scholarship but unfortunately does not retain all the beauty of the earlier translation. In this volume I use my own translations from the Hebrew, which aim at literalness more than style, hoping to let the original words speak more directly to us.

I am grateful to Phillip Ratner for allowing me to join him in bringing something of the inner spirit of the Psalms to you and thousands of others through these pages. I hope the hours you spend with this volume will prove a time of blessing beyond all your expectations.

Blessed Are They

Psalm I

1 Blessed are they who enter not the assembly of
   the ungodly,
   nor stand in the gathering of sinners, nor sit with
   the scornful.
2 Their delight is in the Law of the Lord;
   day and night they meditate upon it.
3 They shall be like a tree planted by rivers of water.
   They bring forth their fruit in due season;
   their leaves shall not wither.
   Whatever they produce is good.
4 Not so the ungodly.
   They are like the chaff that the wind drives away.
5 They, as evildoers, shall not stand in the judgment,
   nor, as sinners, have a place in the congregation of the
   just ones.
6 The Lord watches over the way of the just
   but the assembly of the ungodly shall perish.

Their delight is in the law of the Lord;
day and night they meditate upon it.
They shall be like a tree planted by rivers of water.
They bring forth their fruit in due season;
their leaves shall not wither.

Blessed Are They

"Blessed are they." The whole tone of the inspired collection of wisdom songs we call Psalms is set in this little song, placed at the head. A prologue, as it were. The Psalms lead us, draw us, guide us into the way that leads to abundant blessings, a truly blessed and happy life.

First, we must make our choice. We are free. We hear again echo down the years that clear directive of the man to whom God spoke face-to-face, holy Moses: "Choose life!" (Deut. 30:19).

If we want a blessed life we cannot seek our friends and companions among those who want to pursue other ways, ways unworthy of those who are made to share divine life. We cannot spend our time listening to them, be it in passing conversations or on the television or radio. We need to garner our time so that we can be enlightened by the words that will guide us to walk in the way of the Lord, the way of true and lasting blessedness.

The Law of the Lord, Torah, God's inspired Word, promises life even as it directs it. It promises all the fullness of life to those who live it fully. But only to those who open themselves to its fullness. Hence, day and night we want to make time to take the Scriptures in hand and seek by serious, personal reflection to let their wisdom become the sap of our lives.

Benedict of Nursia, the great wise man of the West, has his disciples arise after the middle of the night, each night, to use its last, quietest, deepest hours to meditate upon the Law of the Lord as it is laid out, first of all, in the Psalms and then in the other Scriptures. Again at dawn, through the day, and at evening till they close the day, his disciples are to have the Psalms on their lips, forming their minds and hearts. Any who have done this, who have meditated upon the Law of the Lord day and night, know what a delight this saving Word becomes. It endows the whole of life with meaning and hope. I delight in the Law of the Lord because it shows me the sure way to come to the full realization of all the deepest aspirations of my being. My life is animated and made green with hope. It even, by God's mercy, produces abundant fruit. Indeed, the fruit is in abundance, and comes forth directly from the provident hands of God, even while I am allowed to enjoy the sweet repose of meditation. And there is always promise of more. For the very flow of wisdom is ours, the sapiential sap that enlivens our every outreach and causes them to flower, delighting all who behold them and bearing fruit for them. The wise one, whose wisdom comes from the Word of God, is a joy to the people.

It is with the rich promise of the first Psalm, Blessed Are They, that we enter the Psalter, knowing that the time we spend with it—be it during the quiet of the night or the pauses in the midst of the labors of the day—will be among the most fruitful of our lives. The fruit of mediation on the inspired Word of God is a life more like unto God's, a life worthy of the image of God that we are. As we let the Law of the Lord, his inspired Word, guide us, we can confidently rely on the constant watchful care of the Lord. And we will surely come to taste the sweet fruit of our meditation and action and know true delight. What is more, as we face the passing years and know the diminishments of aging, we need never fear withering, losing the fresh greenness of hope, so long as we continue to meditate upon the Law of the Lord day and night.

Blessed, indeed, will we be. For with minds filled, enriched, and expanded by the wisdom of the Psalms, we will not be tempted to follow the advice of the wicked, or take the paths sinners trod, or sit idly with those who are overcome with cynicism. We will delight in the Law of Lord; we will celebrate a truly blessed and happy life.

O Lord, Our Lord

Psalm 8a

1 O Lord, our Lord, how glorious is your name through all
   the earth;
   you have established your glory above the heavens.
   Out of the mouths of infants and babes at the breast
2 you have brought forth praise in the face of your enemies
   that you might silence the hostile and the vengeful.
3 When I consider your heavens, the work of your fingers,
   the moon and the stars, which you have made,
4 what is a human that you are mindful of such,
   the offspring of woman that you care for such?
5 For you have made such a little lower than the angels,
   and have crowned that one with glory and honor....

What is a human that you are mindful of such,
the offspring of woman that you care for such?
For you have made such a little lower than the angels,
and have crowned that one with glory and honor.

WIN A $100 GIFT CERTIFICATE!

Fill in this card and mail it to us— or fill it in **online** at

skylightpaths.com/ feedback.html

—to be eligible for a $100 gift certificate for SkyLight Paths books.

Fill in this card and return it to us to be eligible for our quarterly drawing for a $100 gift certificate for SkyLight Paths books.

We hope that you will enjoy this book and find it useful in enriching your life.

Book title: _____

Your comments: _____

How you learned of this book: _____

If purchased: Bookseller _____ City _____ State _____

Please send me a free SkyLight Paths Publishing catalog. I am interested in: (check all that apply)

1. ❏ Spirituality
2. ❏ Mysticism/Kabbalah
3. ❏ Philosophy/Theology
4. ❏ Spiritual Texts
5. ❏ Religious Traditions (Which ones?)
6. ❏ Children's Books
7. ❏ Prayer/Worship
8. ❏ Meditation
9. ❏ Interfaith Resources

Name (PRINT) _____

Street _____

City _____ State _____ Zip _____

E-MAIL (FOR SPECIAL OFFERS ONLY) _____

Please send a SkyLight Paths Publishing catalog to my friend:

Name (PRINT) _____

Street _____

City _____ State _____ Zip _____

SKYLIGHT PATHS® Publishing Tel: (802) 457-4000 • Fax: (802) 457-4004

Available at better booksellers. Visit us online at www.skylightpaths.com

O Lord, Our Lord

*I*t is good for us to know that the angels hover over us, to
know we have their powerful protection, their loving care,
their wise guidance—if we are open to it. Yet, no matter in how
many ways they are superior to us, they are one with us in this:
we are all the beloved creation of our most beneficent God. And
our greatest dignity and joy is in acknowledging this and giving
voice to it and in all things fulfilling the will of our Creator.

Even when we are painfully aware of our weakness and
vulnerability, it is well for us to remain ever conscious of the
reality that we have indeed been made by a most provident and
loving Creator just a little lower than the angels, crowned with
glory and honor. Yes, crowned—and not just in some future
kingdom but even now—we are the crown of creation,
endowed with reason and the power to love. This is our true
crown: our power to know and to love, for it makes us to be the
very image of God. What glory! What an honor! And what a
responsibility.

Yes, God has "put all things under our feet, all livestock and
cattle, yes, and the beasts of the fields, the birds of the air and
the fishes of the sea and all that passes through the depths of
the seas." God has given us dominion over the works of God's
fingers. We have responsibilities here. Alas, responsibilities to
which we have responded poorly. There is ample place here for
repentance and growth. But it is not here, as stewards of creation, where the crown of our glory essentially resides. It is in
the ever-challenging paradox—which ultimately finds its
supreme expression in the Cross and Resurrection—that in
weakness lies the expression of our greatest strength. It is here

that we are ministers of God's recreating and redeeming grace: "Out of the mouths of infants and babes at the breast you have brought forth praise in the face of your enemies that you might silence the hostile"—all those who would degrade you and us by degrading human dignity and your creative benignity which has so crowned us. With childlike faith, the totally trusting faith of the child, we proclaim you are Creator, the Source of all that is. Let no one deceive us with their false pretensions. With the purity of unadulterated simplicity, we profess and declare that the glory of the Lord fills the earth and reaches beyond the heavens.

"What is a human that you are mindful of such, the offspring of woman that you care for such?" The human person is the delight of your eyes, the crown of your creation. Yes, we have strayed like sheep and your Good Shepherd would carry us safely back to the security of the Community of Love if we would let him. You are the generous Father ever on the watch. You stand ready to rush out to welcome and restore the child who has wasted a heritage in a life of dissipation and sin. We are forgetful of you and all the good you do sustaining the ungrateful. What a blessing when the sinner, coming into self-realization, embraces the dignity of a child of God and turns back to you! There is no jealousy in you our God, who wants only to share with us the divine glory.

No matter what be the wonder and beauty and magnificence of the heavens—and we are ever discovering more—your glory is beyond it. And it is for that glory we are made. To it we are destined. "O Lord, our Lord, how glorious is your name through all the earth!"—and beyond.

You Gave Us Dominion

Psalm 8b

1 O Lord, our Lord, how glorious is your name through all
    the earth;
  you have established your glory above the heavens.
  Out of the mouths of infants and babes at the breast
2 You have brought forth praise in the face of your enemies
  that you might silence the hostile and the vengeful.
3 When I consider your heavens, the work of your fingers,
  the moon and the stars, which you have made,
4 what is a human that you are mindful of such,
  the offspring of woman that you care for such?
5 For you have made such a little lower than the angels,
  and have crowned that one with glory and honor.
6 You gave us dominion over the works of your fingers;
  you put all things under our feet,
7 all livestock and cattle, yes, and the beasts of the fields,
8 the birds of the air and the fishes of the sea
  and all that passes through the depths of the seas.
9   O Lord, our Lord, how glorious is your name through all
    the earth!

You gave us dominion over the works of your fingers;
you put all things under our feet,
all livestock and cattle, yes, and the beasts of the fields,
the birds of the air and the fishes of the sea.

You Gave Us Dominion

What a delightful world it was when it came forth from the fingers of God. All, beasts and humans alike, could be together, enjoying the wonders of creation. A parrot could roost on the idle horn of a bull. A monkey could sit peacefully in mirthful joy even at the feet of a lion, who looked in awe upon the amazing turtle. Yes, the lamb and the lion could huddle close under the eyes of the smirking elephant. A more demure horse, closer to man and woman, could share something of their embarrassment. What is the human, Lord—little, weak, and vulnerable—that you give us dominion over all the wondrous work of your fingers?

We have taken thousands of years and yet we seem to be ever at the beginning of understanding the wonders of your creation: the dancing of protons and neutrons, the fabulous whirling of DNA and of the far galaxies. We are far distant from exercising a wise and benevolent dominion over them, from fully and reasonably participating in the benignity of your creative power. No wonder our first progenitors huddle shyly in the midst of their domain. They and we, in each language, will name this vast array of expressions of your beauty, might and strength, of your tenderness and care.

We have far more reason to cast our eyes down in shame, beholding what we have done and are doing to your wondrous gift and responsibility. Rather than imaging your benignity, we have so often desecrated, marred, and even destroyed wondrous products of your creative Word. We have turned creative forces of good that have served us, all unknowing for millennia, into horrible weapons of mass destruction. We have snuffed out life and desecrated the work of your fingers and the creative accomplishments of sisters and brothers who had used well the gifts you have given us to enhance and celebrate life.

O Lord, how glorious is your name through all the earth! But we do not hear it. You have established your glory above the heavens, and we send our spacecrafts and telescopes to explore. You have warned us, though. If in the midst of the exercise of our dominion we become so taken up with and even inflated by the little share of your wisdom that we have and are able to use, if we do not become as little ones, we cannot enter in and share the true wisdom of the Kingdom of heaven (Matt. 18:3). Out of the mouths of infants and babes at the breast you have brought forth praise in the face of your foes—the insidious pride that alienates from you and the blasphemies that even deny your existence, not to speak of your creative benignity to which we owe all. If we can really see the creation with the open eyes and wonder of a child, we will know our true self and our place in your creation. And it is so wondrous—a little lower than the angels. You have indeed crowned us with glory and honor. Should there not pour forth from our mouths an unceasing flow of praise?

Lord, even as we praise the majesty of your name in all the earth, help us to exercise our stewardship with a full sense of responsibility and true humility. May all the earth be seen as a common heritage for all your children, to be reverenced and shared by all with equity.

O Lord, our Lord, how glorious is your name through all the earth!

The Heavens Declare the Glory of God

Psalm 19

1 The heavens declare the glory of God;
   and the sky manifests God's handiwork.
2 Day after day proclaims it and night after night shows
     it forth.
3 There is no speech, nor language, nor is their voice heard,
4 Yet their proclamation has gone forth through all the earth
   and their message to the end of the world.
   In the heavens has God set up a tent for the sun,
5 which, as a bridegroom, comes out of its chamber,
   delights like a champion to run its course.
6 From one end of the heavens it comes forth
   and it goes out to the other
   and nothing escapes its burning heat.
7 The Law of the Lord is perfect, refreshment for the soul;
   the Decree of the Lord is sure, wisdom for the simple.
8 The Precepts of the Lord are right, joy for the heart;
   the Commandment of the Lord is radiant, light for
     the eyes.

9 The Edict of the Lord is unadulterated, enduring forever;
    the Judgments of the Lord are true, all of them just,
10 more desirable than gold, than much fine gold,
    sweeter than honey, honey from the comb.
11 Your servant is formed by them;
    there is great reward in keeping them.
12 Who can understand one's own sin?
    Cleanse me from my secret faults.
13 Keep your servant from presumption; let it not have
        dominion over me.
    Then shall I be upright and innocent of the great
        transgression.
14 May the words of my mouth and the thoughts of my heart
    be acceptable in your sight, O Lord, my Rock and
        my Redeemer.

The heavens declare the glory of God;
and the sky manifests God's handiwork.

The Heavens Declare the Glory of God

*I*n these wondrous days in which we live, day after day, space telescopes and probes lay out for us ever more fully and wondrously the glories of the creation scattered with such prodigality through time and space. And yet we know we are but touching the hem of God's garment. The heavens declare the glory of God. And even as we go out, we look within: atoms, neutrons, protons, and ever deeper. More wonders! Even if we did not have Torah, the Writings, the Word of God, we would still have in the creation a lifetime and more of reading to delight us and draw us into ever greater wonder. We would still need the Psalms to give us the words that would even begin to worthily voice our response to this message of might and of a mighty love. One wonders how anyone can stand, open-minded, gazing into a starry sky and not experience rising up from the depths of one's being the need to adore.

As wondrous as is the message of the night sky, more appreciated now that we know more of this galaxy and others, it is our great star, the sun, that most impresses. Its commanding march across the heavens makes it the worthy image of the Bridegroom of our souls, the Son of Justice, who illumines our lives with the message of Divine Love and Care with all the graces of healing redemption.

As powerfully eloquent as is the proclamation of the sun, moon, and stars, they have no speech, no language, nor is their voice heard. So the thoughts of the joyful and grateful singer turn to the greater gift: the Word of God. Call it what you will: Law, Decree, Precept, Commandment, Edict, or Judgment, it is perfect. It is refreshment for the soul; sure wisdom; joy for the heart; a radiant light for the eyes; more desirable than gold, than much fine gold; sweeter than honey. We want to be formed by it, observe it, and yet not let any pride take possession of us because of our observance. We want to thank the Lord for giving us the insight and grace to appreciate his most precious gift and the will to observe all that it teaches us. Yet we think of the story Rabbi Jesus once told of the Pharisee and the tax collector who went up to the Temple to pray. The Pharisee thanked the Lord for all the good he did but prided himself on it: "I thank you, God, that I am not grasping, unjust, adulterous like everyone else, and particularly that I am not like this tax collected here. I fast twice a week; I pay tithes on all I get." The tax collector simply humbled himself before God: "God, be merciful to me, a sinner." He was the one who went home justified (Luke 18:10–14). Who can understand his own sin? We humbly ask the Lord to wash us of our hidden faults—even those hidden from ourselves—and preserve us from pride.

This most beautiful Psalm ends with a prayer that we might well append to each Psalm we pray:

> "May the words of my mouth and the thoughts of
>   my heart
>   be acceptable in your sight, O Lord, my Rock and
>   my Redeemer."

In the Psalms, God himself, through the Spirit, inspiring the heart of the poet, has given us not only the words we need to begin to praise God as we ought. God also draws the heart that is open and truly listening into the experience that enables that human heart to pour forth inspired praise as its own. The Lord redeems us from all our sin and pettiness and becomes for us the solid Rock upon which we can establish a firm foundation for a life of prayer, one with the Word, giving due glory to the God whom the heavens and the whole creation declare as truly worthy of our awed obeisance.

May the Lord Hear You

Psalm 20

1 May the Lord hear you in the day of trouble!
  May the name of the God of Jacob protect you!
2 May God send you help from the sanctuary
  and give you support from Zion.
3 May God remember all your offerings
  and consider your burnt sacrifices pleasing.
4 May God grant your heart's desires
  and fulfill all your plans
5 that we may rejoice in your victory
  and in the name of our God set up our banners.
  May the Lord fulfill all your prayers!
6 Now I know that the Lord will help his anointed;
  he will hear him from his holy heaven
  and save him with the strength of his right hand.
7 Some trust in chariots and some in horses
  but we trust in the name of the Lord our God.
8 Our enemies are brought down and fall
  but we rise and stand upright.
9 Give the King victory, O Lord;
  answer when we call.

Some trust in chariots and some in horses
but we trust in the name of the Lord our God.

May the Lord Hear You

*T*here are still many people in this world who depend, if not on plow horses, then on oxen and mules. And there are some who still depend on horse carts. We see them on the side of some of America's great roads in Pennsylvania and Missouri. But when it comes to the might of nations, we depend rather on the products of our munition factories and war laboratories, on computer sciences and satellites. But has any of this brought peace and security? We live now more than ever in terror of terrorism. We have a variety of elaborate plans and programs; we build barriers of all sorts. But in the end we are still painfully aware of our vulnerability. If we are to rise and stand upright and free, we must call upon the Lord.

We have faced the threats of the Cold War, the dangers of great Communist powers. Some nations still "play" with weapons of mass destruction. Wars rage within nations around the globe. And there is constantly the threat of escalation. We now face the more insidious forays of terrorists who can strike us in any place at any time. How can we know any peace of mind and heart in these days of trouble?

With the Psalmist there rises up from the heart of God's People—from our own hearts—a confident prayer. We must be faithful in giving God due honor in prayer and sacrifice, in being a faithful and grateful people. Then not only will we be able to shout in victory, but the Lord, the all-good and all-merciful, will grant us our heart's desires; he will fulfill all our prayers; he will bring peace to this world of ours, where all can live together in harmony and gratitude as one family under God.

Faith, of course, is the key—trusting faith. The Lord will help, he will hear from his holy heaven and he will save us with the strength of his right hand. If we allow the Spirit who formed the heart of the Psalmist to form our own hearts, we can pray with the confidence that brings peace, "We trust in the name of the Lord." Another inspired pen would later write, "For those who love God all things work together unto good." There are times when our only refuge lies in faith and trust.

Let us pray with unwavering confidence. "I know that the Lord will help—he will hear from his holy heaven and save with the strength of his right hand."

O Lord, answer when we call!

The Earth Is the Lord's

Psalm 24

1 The earth is the Lord's, and its fullness,
the world and those who dwell in it.
2 For the Lord has founded it upon the seas,
and established it upon the rivers.
3 Who shall ascend the mountain of the Lord?
Who shall stand in the Holy Place?
4 The one who has clean hands and a pure heart,
who has not worshiped what is false, nor sworn deceitfully.
5 Such a one shall receive a blessing from the Lord
and righteousness from the God of our salvation.
6 Such is the company of those who seek the Lord,
who seek the face of the God of Jacob.
7 Lift up your heads, O gates! Be lifted up, you ancient doors!
And the King of glory shall come in.
8 Who is this King of glory?
The Lord strong and mighty, the Lord mighty in battle.
9 Lift up your heads, O gates! Be lifted up, you
ancient doors!
And the King of glory shall come in.
10 Who is this King of glory?
The Lord of hosts, he is the King of glory.

Who shall ascend the mountain of the Lord?
Who shall stand in the Holy Place?
The one who has clean hands and a pure heart.

The Earth Is the Lord's

Even before (remember the ill-fated attempt to build a tower to heaven at Babel in Gen. 11:4–8?) but certainly since Moses ascended Mount Sinai, we think of going to the heights to encounter the living God. Christ seems to confirm this. He ascends a mountain to inaugurate his own proclamation that the kingdom of God is at hand (Matt. 5:1). Later he takes Peter, James, and John and leads them up a high mountain, the one we identify today as Mount Tabor, in order to strengthen them with a revelation of his glory, drawing them into the cloud of Divine Presence. Wondrous as was the experience, it still left the three disciples sprawling in fearsome awe. Yet the encounter of the New Covenant still lay ahead, as the great Lawgiver and the great Prophet of the Hebrew Covenant reminded Jesus in this moment of glory on Tabor. The Son, in whom God was well pleased, had yet to face the wrath of God, not in thunder and lightning as Moses on Sinai but in the brutality and darkness of Mount Calvary.

"Who shall ascend the mountain of the Lord? Who shall stand in the Holy Place?" Moses, indeed, had clean hands and a pure compassionate heart as did Christ the Lord. If we would ascend the heights, spiritually more than physically, to experience the living God and know God's all-embracing love, we, too, must have clean hands and a pure heart.

Indeed, "The earth is the Lord's, and its fullness, the world and those who dwell in it." It is not necessary to leave the world and to ascend to the heights. The Lord is present everywhere. If we have but clean hands and pure hearts we can see the Lord in the plain and on the sea, just as much as atop a mountain.

"Blessed are the pure of heart, for they shall see God" (Matt. 5:8). But the climb that confronts the climber, that lay before Moses at Sinai and the three at Tabor, symbolizes the effort we poor sinners have to undertake to achieve this purity. Indeed, the heights are lost in the clouds; the cloud comes down as it did on Sinai to envelop Moses and on Tabor to embrace the three disciples. To encounter the Lord we have to be willing to let go, at least for the moment, of all concern for the things of earth. We have to be of "the company of those who seek the Lord, who seek the face of the God of Jacob."

And more, we must be willing to open ourselves totally to the divine invasion, no matter what fear it evokes in our poor little selves that still want to be masters of the situation. Peter cried, "Lord, it is good for us to be here!" while he still thought he could take command and do something: "Let us build...." But within the cloud we can only surrender to the Awesome. We have to do what we can: lift up our heads to open to the Lord. But then realizing our impotence, we have to let ourselves be lifted up and totally opened so that the King of glory, the Lord strong and mighty, the Lord mighty in battle, can enter in.

As we take up this Psalm, we may sense ourselves still at the foot of the mountain with the long climb and the shrouded heights ahead. We need to lift up our hope and desire to set out on the journey. The Psalms place in our hands a strong staff. If we lean on them in daily meditation, our strength will not flag. We will keep our hands clean and seek a pure heart and stead-fastly ascend the mountain of the Lord and come to stand in the Holy Place.

Judge Me, O Lord

Psalm 26

1 Judge me, O Lord, for I have walked in integrity.
   I have trusted in the Lord without wavering.
2 Examine me, O Lord, and test me;
   test my inmost being and my heart.
3 For your loving kindness is ever before my eyes
   and I have walked in your truth.
4 I have not sat with the worthless,
   nor have I consorted with hypocrites.
5 I have hated the gatherings of evildoers,
   and have not sat with the wicked.
6 I will wash my hands in innocence
   that I may I walk around your altar, O Lord,
7 that I may give voice to thanksgiving
   and tell of all your wondrous works.
8 Lord, I have loved the house in which you dwell,
   the place where your glory abides.

9 Gather not my soul with sinners,
  nor my life with bloodthirsty men
10 in whose hands is evil doing;
  their right hand is full of bribes.
11 But as for me, I will walk in integrity.
  Redeem me and show me your mercy.
12 My foot stands on a level place,
  in the gathering will I bless the Lord.

In the gathering will I bless the Lord.

Judge Me, O Lord

*I*n the gathering will I bless the Lord."

Several times in the day and once in the night I join my community in choir and we chant these powerful, grace-filled songs of the Lord. But something more than mere physical presence in the gathering is called for here. Truly, I must be in the community—one in mind and heart with these, my sisters and brothers. I need to have a profound sense that as we stand before God, the Almighty sees a People, God's Chosen People, made intimately one under the headship of the Christ. We do not stand alone before the Lord. We are his people, the sheep of his flock.

But what does it mean to bless the Lord? We bless one another, calling down God's blessings upon ourselves and others and upon all we have and use. But surely I do not bless God in this way. No, I bless the Lord when I praise the Lord, thank the Lord, acknowledge the Lord as the source of all that is. It is not enough to do this only in words, no matter how holy or inspired they be—not even with the Psalms themselves. This blessing must be the fruit of a life of integrity. I must walk in faithfulness and wash my hands in innocence. Then I can truly bless the Lord and "give voice to thanksgiving and tell of all his wondrous works."

I must confess that it is with a great deal of fear and trepidation that I dare say, "Judge me, O Lord." I cannot say, "I have walked in integrity." Too many painful memories rise up to accuse me. "I am a sinful man, the son of a sinful mother" (Ps. 51:7). I know the burden of my guilt, and it weighs upon me because I have not trusted in the Lord without wavering.

Rightly do I quaver as we pray, "Examine me, O Lord, and test me; test my inmost being and my heart." I know where I have failed in steadfast love and faithfulness. But there is one great fact that makes all the difference, that enables me to dare pray, "Judge me, O Lord." God's "loving kindness is ever before my eyes." We have a Redeemer. This is the truth we now walk in. With the Psalmist we can at every moment cry, "Now I begin." (Ps. 76:10 Vul.). We can let all the burdens of the past be lifted from our shoulders and be shouldered by the Crucified. We can be washed—not only my hands but my whole being—in the blood of the Innocent One. From henceforth I will avoid the gatherings of evildoers; I will not sit with the wicked.

To this we are called: to join the gathering in the eternal Jerusalem and bless the Lord; to give God unceasing praise by the witness of a blameless life, a life made blameless by the loving kindness of God, our Redeemer. Even now we prepare for this and, to some extent, enter into it when we gather to bless the Lord. That is why I love the house in which the Lord dwells, the place where his glory abides. He has promised, "Wherever two or three gather in my name, there I am in the midst" (Matt. 18:20). Redeemed by the lovingkindness of God, gathered into the holy community as his Chosen People, I can pray there, "Judge me, O Lord," for I walked now in a God-given, supported integrity. With good reason I will "give voice to thanksgiving and tell of your wondrous works."

"In the gathering will I bless the Lord."

The Lord Is My Light

Psalm 27

1 The Lord is my light and my salvation; whom shall I fear?
  The Lord is the strength of my life; of whom shall I
    be afraid?
2 When the wicked come upon me to eat up my flesh,
  They, my enemies and my foes, shall stumble and fall.
3 Though an army should encamp against me, my heart
    shall not fear;
  though they should war against me, even then will I
    be confident.
4 One thing have I asked of the Lord; this will I seek:
  that I may dwell in the house of the Lord all the days of
    my life,
  to behold the beauty of the Lord and to be in his Temple.
5 For in the time of trouble he shall hide me in his tent;
  in the secret places of his dwelling shall he hide me;
  he shall set me high upon a rock.
6 Then shall my head be lifted up above my enemies round
    about me.
  I will offer in the Lord's tabernacle sacrifices of joy;
  I will sing, yes, I will sing praises unto the Lord.

7 Hear, O Lord, when I cry aloud!
   Have mercy upon me and answer me.
8 When you said, "Seek my face,"
   my heart said to you, "Your face, Lord, will I seek."
9 Hide not your face far from me;
   put not your servant away in anger.
   You have been my help;
   leave me not, never forsake me, O God of my salvation.
10 Though my father and my mother forsake me,
   the Lord will take me to himself.
11 Teach me your way, O Lord,
   and lead me on an even path because of my enemies.
12 Deliver me not over to the will of my enemies;
   for false witnesses rise up against me, breathing out cruelty.
13 I would not have survived, if I had not believed
   that I would see the goodness of the Lord in the land of
      the living.
14 Wait on the Lord; be of good courage, and he shall
      strengthen your heart.
   Wait, I say, wait on the Lord!

Though an army should encamp against me,
my heart shall not fear;
though they should war against me,
even then will I be confident.

The Lord Is My Light

*T*his is my favorite Psalm. It speaks most directly to me and my life. It resonates most profoundly in my heart. It is the story of my vocation: "When you said, 'Seek my face,' my heart said to you, 'Your face, Lord, will I seek.'" The deepest and most profound prayer that ever arises from my heart: "Hide not your face from me; put not your servant away in anger."

Because of serious health complications, I was born prematurely and my mother could not attend to me. Psychologists would assure me that this lack of maternal care marks my whole life. My father died while I was still very young and, as any child would, I experienced this as abandonment. "Though my father and my mother forsake me, the Lord will take me to himself." Later in life "false witnesses have risen up against me." Indeed, "I would not have survived, if I had not believed that I would see the goodness of the Lord in the land of the living." I live now under the tutelage of a great spiritual master, Benedict of Nursia. The last words this great saint wrote were: "Through patience we share in the passion of Christ"—and come to the glory of his resurrection. So "wait on the Lord; be of good courage, and he shall strengthen your heart. Wait, I say, wait on the Lord!"

This Psalm brings to mind one of the first great days of the future King David, the attributable author of the earliest Psalms. A small, weak Israelite army stood quaking in the face of the superior Philistine forces. With arrogant boast the pagans challenged the Chosen of God. Only the inspired youth was ready to stand up to alien might. "Though an army should encamp against me, my heart shall not fear; though they should war against me, even then will I be confident." Not trusting in sword or spear but in his God-given strength and skill, with God's help and daring he slew the towering boast of the enemy and sent the dismayed army fleeing in a disorderly retreat. "The Lord is my light and my salvation; whom shall I fear? The Lord is the strength of my life; of whom shall I be afraid?"

And what did this young man seek in his purity of heart? "One thing have I asked of the Lord; this will I seek: that I may dwell in the house of the Lord all the days of my life, to behold the beauty of the Lord and to be in his Temple."

Humble is the prayer he gives us here. Powerful and victorious though he was, he cries for pity, for help: "Leave me not, never forsake me, O God of my salvation." And he prays with confidence, "Though my father and my mother forsake me, the Lord will take me to himself." Indeed this inspired man of the Sinai Covenant seems to reach beyond his times and revelation and put faith in life eternal: "I would not have survived, if I had not believed that I would see the goodness of the Lord in the land of the living." The God of his heart had said to him, "Seek my face," and he responded, "Your face, Lord, will I seek. Hide not your face from me." And with total confidence, wise and lyrical, he counsels us, "Wait on the Lord; be of good courage, and he shall strengthen your heart. Wait, I say, wait on the Lord!"

We can be strong and bold and full of hope when our heart is pure and we seek one thing: to live in the house of the Lord all our days, in the house of his good will, in his love, in the embrace of his loving Presence.

Lord, you say to me, "Seek my face." And with all my heart I say to you, "Your face, Lord, do I seek." "You are my light," the beacon light of gentle, powerful, burning love that says, "I desire you." And my whole, empty, starving, thirsting, longing being seeks only this, its all-satisfying Light of Love.

I Will Extol You, O Lord

Psalm 30

1 I will extol you, O Lord, for you have lifted me up
   and have not let my foes rejoice over me.
2 O Lord my God, I cried to you and you have healed me.
3 O Lord, you have brought up my soul from the grave,
   you have kept me alive that I should not go down to the pit.
4 Sing unto the Lord, O you his saints,
   and give thanks to his holy name.
5 For the Lord's anger endures but a moment; his favor
      for life;
   weeping may endure for a night, but joy comes in
      the morning.
6 In my prosperity I said, "I shall never be moved."
7 Lord, by your favor you have made me as strong as
      a mountain;
   but when you hid your face, I was troubled.
8 I cried to you, O Lord;
   to the Lord I made supplication:
9 "What profit is there in my blood, when I go down to
      the pit?
   Shall the dust praise you? Shall it declare your fidelity?

10 Hear, O Lord, and have mercy upon me;
    Lord, be my helper!"
11 You have turned my mourning into dancing;
    you ripped off my sackcloth and girded me with gladness,
12 that I may sing praise to you and not be silent.
    O Lord my God, I will thank you forever.

You have turned my mourning into dancing;
you ripped off my sackcloth and girded me with gladness.

I Will Extol You, O Lord

There are those moments, those wonderful moments when all of life's burdens seem suddenly to disappear. It even happens when I am in the deepest mourning and the Lord in his love and mercy suddenly touches me. What is it? I don't really know. But God in his goodness gives joy even to the depths of my sorrow, to my very being. For a moment I know God is God and God is my God.

God is joy, beatific joy. And it is for God that I am made. God made us to know God; for this we have a mind with infinite capacity. We want then nothing more than to be one with God, to serve God, to be of service in God's great creation project that has no other end or purpose save that we share in the joy of the Lord.

If there is any sorrow—and has there ever been a sorrow as great as that of God himself in the Passion and death of Jesus?—it is all because we have not believed in the benignity of the Creator and have thought we knew better than God the way to our happiness and acted accordingly. And we continue to fail to believe and strike out on our own into the ways that lead to mourning and death.

When we wake to our folly, when we turn back to God, when we don our sackcloth of repentance, God rips off our sackcloth with savage love and girds us with gladness! Why? So that we might sing praise to God and not be silent. It is in joyful praise, we find our fulfillment. "Sing unto the Lord, O you his saints, and give thanks to his holy name."

We want to extol the Lord, sing his praises. He has drawn us up out of nothingness into being and life. "Sing unto the Lord, O you his saints, and give thanks to his holy name. For the Lord's anger endures but a moment, his favor for life." We have but to turn back to God and the dark night of sin with its mourning turns into morning joy.

The Gospel of Joy, the Good News, is difficult for us to accept. Such gratuitous goodness is not the common human experience. An unmitigated joy seems the lot of fools divorced from reality, not the lot of those who live in this world so marked by human malice and natural disaster. (Perhaps not so natural— someday we may come to see that all so-called natural disasters are the result of the ways we have abused the creation in our faulty selfish stewardship.) Even looking upon the crucifix: this is the Father's beloved Son in whom he is well pleased. How can we believe that this is the God of Joy who has made us for joy, who would rip off our sackcloth and gird us with joy? The answer always lies beyond. Behind Calvary is the Garden where Eden was healed in the Resurrection. Behind every crucifixion, even in this most bitter, over the hill lies the joy beyond all expectation. Only to the extent that we know the bitter, binding sorrow of Calvary can we know the exuberant transforming joy of Easter. The promise of a Promised Land was fulfilled only through the slavery of Egypt and the Passover. The end, if we are willing to let the Word form and shape our hearts, is always the fulfillment of all the promises of Eden, of Noah, of Abraham, and of Christ himself—a full participation in the unending joy of the Lord.

There is no room for presumption here. In the time of prosperity we dare not say, "I shall never be moved." It is only as long as we humbly keep hold of the fact that it is by the Lord's favor that we stand fast, will we stand fast. If the Lord hides his face, we will be troubled and worse. Yet God is ever ready to hear our cry for help and be gracious, in the full sense of the word. By God's grace we are saved from all our follies and brought into the joy God always wants for us. So let us sing praise to the Lord and not be silent. Let us thank our God forever.

I Will Bless the Lord

Psalm 34

1 I will bless the Lord at all times; his praise shall continually
   be in my mouth.

2 My soul shall boast in the Lord; the humble shall hear and
   be glad.

3 Glorify the Lord with me, together let us extol his name.

4 I sought the Lord, and he heard me and delivered me from
   all my fears.

5 Look to the Lord and be enlightened; then you will never
   be ashamed.

6 This poor one cried and was heard by the Lord
   and was saved from every trouble.

7 The angel of the Lord camps round about those who fear
   him, and delivers them.

8 O taste and see that the Lord is good; blessed is the one
   who trusts in him!

9 Fear the Lord, you his saints! For those who fear him suffer
   no want.

10 The rich will suffer want and hunger,
   but those who seek the Lord shall not want for any
   thing good.

11 Come, children, listen to me; I will teach you fear of
 the Lord.
12 Which of you desires life and wants many days to enjoy
 the good?
13 Keep your tongue from evil and your lips from
 speaking deceit.
14 Shun evil and do good; seek peace and pursue it.
15 The eyes of the Lord are upon the righteous and his ears
 are open to their cry.
16 The face of the Lord is against those who do evil,
 to cut off remembrance of them from the earth.
17 The righteous cry and the Lord hears and delivers them
 from all their troubles.
18 The Lord is near to the broken hearted and saves those
 crushed in spirit.
19 Many are the afflictions of the good,
 but the Lord delivers them from them all.
20 The Lord protects all their bones; not one of them
 is broken.
21 Evil shall slay the wicked and those who hate the good
 shall perish.
22 The Lord redeems his servants; no one who trusts in the
 Lord shall perish.

Keep your tongue from evil
and your lips from speaking deceit.

I Will Bless the Lord

We are summoned by Wisdom: "Come, children, listen to me; I will teach you fear of the Lord." The summons is to those of us who desire life, want to be truly alive in the Lord, to enjoy days unending, to enjoy the Good—for one is good: God (Luke 18:19).

Here is the way to acquire what we seek: "Keep your tongue from evil and your lips from speaking deceit." James, the brother of the Lord, wrote to the first Christian communities, "If anyone does not fall short in speech, that one is a perfect man, able to bridle the whole body" (James 3:2). It might be easier, indeed, to put our hands over our mouths and never speak a word. "The wise are known by the fewness of their words." But even the wisest must say something. And these words must be carefully guarded. It is so easy to slip into exaggeration, to color the truth, to embellish the story, even when we have no desire to deceive.

We will not succeed in shunning evil if we do not have a passion to do good, if we do not truly seek peace and pursue it positively with true commitment. Peace is the tranquility that enters our own hearts when our lives are well ordered. When we strive for this, the eyes of the Lord will be upon us and his ears will be open to our cry. Peace comes to nations when justice prevails. So long as injustice prevails there cannot be peace within nations or among nations. Justice must begin with recognition that God is God, Lord and Creator of all. We are all stewards given responsibility to care for the creation and to share this creation in a way that every human person has at least a reasonable opportunity to live a fully human life—that a certain equity prevails among the beneficiaries of God's largess. God will deliver us from all our troubles. God will be near to us when we are broken-hearted and crushed in spirit. We may have to suffer much, but God will save us from all. We will never be lost.

By the powerful working of the Spirit who inspired them and through them inspires us, the Psalms form in our minds and hearts the attitudes that are worthy of the Chosen Ones and are conducive to the fullness of life to which we are called. The Psalmist rightly begins his Psalm by speaking of his relation with God. For it is only if our relationship with God is what it should be that our relationship with one another will be one of truth, justice, and peace.

To God is due praise, gratitude, and acknowledgment that God is the source of all—to God belongs glory and honor. From God we learn the true order of things, we look to the Lord and we are enlightened. We will learn due fear and reverence, a reverence that will extend to all God's creation—the true basis for justice.

But God's design for us is far more than this. "Taste and see." God would have us experience, in a most human and intimate way, the goodness of God. More than hearing or seeing, touching or smelling, tasting brings the experience within the human person. When we come to so savor the goodness of God, then complete trust almost necessarily follows along with a wholehearted desire to embrace the divine order of things, the ultimate source and criteria for justice and peace.

If we taste and see how good God is then we will indeed bless the Lord at all times. We will keep our tongues from evil; we will seek peace and pursue it. Our desire for life will be fulfilled in all its fullness; we will enjoy the Good, our good God.

As the Hart Longs

Psalm 42

1 As the hart longs for flowing water,
    so my soul longs for you, O God.
2 My soul thirsts for God, for the living God;
    when shall I drink in the Presence of God?
3 My tears have been my food day and night,
    when people were saying to me all day long, "Where is
      your God?"
4 I remember these things as I pour out my soul:
    I went with the multitude;
    I led them to the house of God
    with shouts of joy and praise,
    with the multitude that kept the holyday.
5 Why are you cast down, my soul? And why are
      you restless?
    Hope in God, for I shall yet praise him, my Help, my
      present God.
6 O my God, my soul is cast down within me because I
      remember you
    from the land of Jordan and Hermon, from the hill
      of Mizar.

7 Deep calls unto deep at the sound of your cataracts;
   all your waves and your torrents have gone over me.
8 In the daytime the Lord will rule with loving kindness
   and in the night his song shall be with me.
   My prayer is to the God of my life.
9 I will say to God, my Rock, "Why have you forgotten me?
   Why do I go mourning oppressed by the enemy?"
10 I am as one with a sword thrust in him;
   my enemies oppress me, saying to me all day long, "Where
   is your God?"
11 Why are you cast down, my soul? And why are you restless
   within me?
   Hope in God, for I shall yet praise God, my Help, my
   present God.

As the hart longs for flowing water,
so my soul longs for you, O God.

As the Hart Longs

*M*ost of us probably have never seen a thirsty hart. But having seen a thirsty dog and having known, at one time or another, our own desperate thirst, the image can speak to us. Yet it is only an image that bespeaks a deeper thirst we all have but, alas, are not always in touch with or do not identify. It is the deep thirst that we have, rising from the very depths of our being: a thirst for God. We may experience it more as a restlessness; as Saint Augustine wrote, "Our hearts are made for you, O Lord, and they will not rest until they rest in you." It is only when we are willing to let all our doing and striving go, at least for a bit, and seek to rest quietly before the Lord, that we get in touch with how much we long for the living God. It is then that this beautiful Psalm rises from the depths of our being: "Deep calls unto deep...."

"I remember"—yes in a very real way—I remember "I went with the multitude, I led them to the house of God, with shouts of joy and praise, with the multitude that kept the holy-day." Among some of my happiest memories are those of great liturgical moments, moments when I celebrated God's special blessings on my life: my consecration as a monk, my blessing as an abbot, the jubilee of my ordination. And the moments when we simply celebrated God's own great goodness, the mysteries of Christ, and the outpouring of the Spirit.

When my heart has been formed by the Lord through the inspiration of his inspired singer, the holy Psalmist—it is then that "my prayer is to the God of my life."

This is not to deny that there are those truly dark nights, when God seems very far away indeed or almost non-existent.

Then I cry out to God with the Psalmist, "Why have you forgotten me? Why do I go mourning oppressed by the enemy?" Oppressive thoughts and feelings beset me in the emptiness. The worst alleged against me is shouted within by my own spirit, so violent that it seems a sword thrust in me. It is then by God's grace I realize that I must challenge my own soul: "Why are you cast down, my soul? And why are you restless within me?" Faith and movement of the Spirit, from deep within me, makes the Psalm's command a burning and empowered Word for me: "Hope in God." Under the powerful influence of the living Word who gives me word and spirit in these inspired mysteries, "I shall yet praise God, my Help, my present God." Yes, God is present, effectively made present within me when I allow the Psalms to become my word and song.

This prayer rises from the deepest recesses of my being. It sums up my deepest aspirations. It is a prayer filled with hope. It looks forward to fulfillment. It is only a matter of time when all my longing and thirsting shall be slaked, and I shall drink in the Presence of God.

At the entrance of her headquarters in Calcutta, Mother Teresa had a large image of the Crucified painted on the wall with the caption, "I thirst," to remind all that it is not only we who thirst with longing. God thirsts, longing for us and our love. At the same time Mother had added to the tableau the words, "I quench." In a stream that flows out of the pierced heart of Christ we will find the flowing water for which we long, the fullest and most complete human expression of the Love that is God. Jesus said of one occasion, "The one who drinks of this water will yet thirst" (John 4:13). May we ever, indeed, thirst for the flowing water that is the living God.

God Is Our Refuge and Strength

Psalm 46

1 God is our refuge and strength, a very present help in
    times of trouble.
2 Therefore we will not fear though the earth be shaken,
    though the mountains be cast into the midst of the sea,
3 though its waters roar and crash,
    though the mountains shake with its uproar.
4 There is a river, whose streams gladden the city of God,
    the holy place of the tabernacle of the Most High.
5 God is in the midst of the city, it shall not be toppled;
    God shall help it in the dawning of the day.
6 The heathens rage, kingdoms are overturned;
    God speaks out, the earth melts.
7 The Lord of hosts is with us; the God of Jacob is
    our stronghold.
8 Come, behold the works of the Lord,
    see what he has wrought upon the earth.

9 He makes wars to cease throughout the earth;
   he breaks the bow and shatters the spear;
   he burns the chariots with fire.
10 Be still and know that I am God;
   exalted above the nations,
   exalted on the earth.
11 The Lord of hosts is with us; the God of Jacob is
   our stronghold.

Come, behold the works of the Lord,
see what he has wrought upon the earth.
He makes wars to cease throughout the earth;
he breaks the bow and shatters the spear;
he burns the chariots with fire.

God Is Our Refuge and Strength

*A*t first it might incite fear. So much fire, wreckage, havoc. It is the end of something.

The Lord may not actually burn chariots in these days of ours. But how much we need the Lord's help to embrace with our hearts, in spite of our fears, our responsibility to destroy all our weaponry and turn all our wondrous technology into a technology of peace. Our creative genius is meant to better the living conditions of every human person, not bring havoc and destruction. Such a shift is absolutely essential if we would preserve our planet as a healthy, life-supporting environment. Would to God we could truly sing out, "He makes wars to cease throughout the earth." But as long as we use our God-given freedom and the rich resources God has given us in human genius and natural resources to produce incredibly destructive weapons and wage war against our sisters and brothers, we will not be able to behold the works of the Lord. Rather we will see only clouds of smoke arising from ruins, the horror of the atomic mushroom, and the ever-increasing smog of our pollution.

Today, post the tsunami of December 2004, as we take up this Psalm we cannot but have crash in upon us the terrible scenes of that tragedy and its aftermath: "the earth shakes … and mountains are cast into the midst of the sea … its waters roar and crash … the mountains shake with its uproar." A natural phenomenon? We can question if our atomic experiments, the most recent on a South Pacific atoll, have not brought about this cataclysmic shifting of the earth's plates. We can ask, too, if we had used our technology with more wisdom, would we not have had systems in place to warn us of the impending threat. Would we not have developed the means of directing and quieting the great surges of the sea before they swept across the populated coastlands?

"There is a river, whose streams gladden the city of God"—what a different picture this is. It is the river of divine grace, and it calls us to "seek peace and pursue it" (Ps. 34:14). Let us listen to what our God of peace would do: "God is in the midst of the city, it shall not be toppled. (Think of the pictures of the towns on the shores of Sumatra and Sri Lanka.) God shall help it at the dawning of the day.... The Lord makes wars to cease throughout the earth; he breaks the bow and shatters the spear; he burns the chariots with fire."

God is within—within our cities, within our communities and families, within our hearts. Let us turn within and get in touch with this God of might who is a God of love. Getting in touch with our true self, the self that is one with all others, we can find a peace that can only rejoice that the Lord burns our chariots of war, that he makes war to cease to the ends of the earth, that he needs us to use our genius to create a better world for everyone.

As long as we seek to create a false identity of power and possession, to aggrandize ourselves by the production of weaponry, to display our might by crushing others, then mothers and wise elders may cry: Peace! Peace! But there will be no peace. "The Lord of hosts is with us"—on our side, but we are not on the Lord's side. We should not be surprised then that the earth is shaken, that mountains are cast into the midst of the sea and its waters roar and crash. We live with and will continue to live with the consequences of our violence, our abysmal failures to be good stewards of the beautiful earth that the Lord has given us, an earth so delicately balanced to foster and preserve human life.

Yes, it is time for us to be still and know that God is God, "exalted above the nations, exalted on the earth." May the God of peace, indeed, destroy all our proclivity toward war and turn us all into his ways of peace. "The Lord of hosts is with us; the God of Jacob is our stronghold."

Give Ear to My Prayer

Psalm 55a

1 Give ear to my prayer, O God,
  and hide not yourself from my supplication.
2 Pay attention to me and hear me.
  I am overcome with troubles and distraught
3 because of the shouts of the enemy,
  because of the oppression of the wicked,
  for they heap invectives upon me and in their anger they
    hate me.
4 My heart is sorely pained within me
  and the terrors of death come upon me.
5 Fearfulness and trembling have come upon me
  and horror overwhelms me.
6 I cry, "Oh, that I had wings like a dove!
  For then would I fly away and be at rest.
7 Yes, I would fly far away and settle in the wilderness;
8 I would hasten my escape from the raging storm and
    the tempest."
9 Confound them, Lord, divide their speech!
  for I see violence and strife in the city.
10 Day and night they go about upon its walls;
  evil and sorrow are in its midst.

11 Wickedness is in its midst;
   deceit and guile depart not from its streets....
22 Cast your burden upon the Lord and he shall sustain you.
   God shall never allow a good person to be overcome.
23 You, O God, shall bring them down into the pit
      of destruction;
   bloody and deceitful men shall not live out half their days.
   But I will trust in you.

Oh, that I had wings like a dove!

Give Ear to My Prayer

We all have had moments when we wished we could get away from it all. Our thoughts might not have been as poetic as our Psalmist's: "Oh, that I had wings like a dove," but we did want to "fly away and be at rest."

We are rightly horrified by the pictures of the terrible sufferings of our sisters and brothers that enter our homes and our hearts. We will never forget the devastation of the tsunami of December 2004, the terrorism of 9/11, or the daily horrors being wrought upon the victims of terrorism around the world. But we do not have to go so far or into the past. In our own affluent society, the rich get richer and the poor get poorer; children suffer malnutrition and abuse; the old are warehoused; the victims of war are left in veterans' hospitals to wait out whatever remains of their lives. Some corporate crime is uncovered and mildly punished, but for the most part such crime mocks the adage, crime does not pay. Political and corporate dishonesty is so prevalent that it is almost accepted as the norm and doesn't disturb the perpetrators' consciences, while migrants work like slaves and others cannot find employment.

But sometimes even all this pain and suffering and human misery gets blocked out by our own personal sufferings. Sickness, poverty, and insecurity are bad enough, but they can perhaps be more easily measured by the plight of others. It is when personal venom, even betrayal, are heaped upon us that our spirit is crushed: "the terrors of death come upon me."

Yes, we would like to get away from it all. "I am over come with trouble and distraught.... My heart is sorely pained within me.... Yes, I would fly away and settle in the wilderness."

How wonderful it would be to have great wings and be able to rise above it all and fly far away. But, in truth, can I really get away from it? No matter what solitude I find, I bring with me my own troubled spirit. I am woven into the fabric of humanity. I cannot cut myself off from the sorrows and pains in my own life or anyone else's.

It is fanciful to think of having great wings—even the wings of a peaceful dove who knows how to settle in the crags in the rocks and welcome the day with its peaceful cooing. Yet, we can—and if we are wise, we will—take refuge in meditation regularly, in the morning and evening, cooing our prayer word, resting in the Divine Love. "Be still and know that I am God." In these moments of restful communion we do "fly away and … rest."

The Psalmist knows that our only hope and refuge is in God. "Give ear to my prayer, O God, hide not yourself." With sure confidence—"I will trust in you"—he advises us: "Cast your burden upon the Lord and he shall sustain you" (1 Pet. 5:7). Meditation and prayer are our refuge and strength. They are two great means that carry us into the realms of peace and confident security where we know "God shall never allow a good person to be overcome."

It Was Not an Enemy

Psalm 55b

12 It was not an enemy who reproached me,
   otherwise I could have borne it.
   Nor was it he who hated me that rose up against me,
   or I would have hid myself from him.
13 But it was you, a man of my rank, my companion
      and confidant.
14 We took sweet counsel together
   and walked together in the house of God.
15 Let the death come upon them;
   let them go down alive to Sheol;
      for evil is in their homes and in their hearts.
16 As for me, I will call upon God and the Lord shall save me.
17 Evening and morning and at noon I will pray and
      cry aloud
   and God shall hear my voice.
18 God will give my soul peace, delivered from the battle,
   for there are many against me.
19 God shall hear and will humble them, the God who abides
      from of old,
   because they have not changed, they fear not God.

20 My companion has turned against one who was at peace
   with him;

   he has broken his covenant.
21 The words of his mouth were smoother than butter,
   but war was in his heart;
   his words were softer than oil,
   yet they were drawn swords.
22 Cast your burden upon the Lord and he shall sustain you.
   God shall never allow a good person to be overcome.
23 You, O God, shall bring them down into the pit
      of destruction;
   bloody and deceitful men shall not live out half their days.
   But I will trust in you.

We took sweet counsel together
and walked together in the house of God.

It Was Not an Enemy

I do not think there is anything "sweeter" than a real communion of spirits, be it between spouses in marriage, brothers or sisters in community, or simply comrades on the journey—those wonderful friendships that saw us through our college years and remain ever nourishingly present in the background through the years that follow. This communion is fullest and approaches a certain completeness when it is grounded in sharing our friendship in the Lord, bringing to each other love and compassion. We are made for infinite, unlimited love. We seek that from our spouses and our friends. But our quest is destined to be frustrated unless our loved one is able to bring to us the love of the Lord, for the Divine Love alone can ultimately satisfy. When we walk, if not literally at least always spiritually, with the crowd in the house of God, then our own love is permeated with the love that leads us sweetly in our common understanding and celebration of life.

No matter how strongly we are bonded in love, life can and will still have its bitterness at times. But with love, companionship, a shoulder to cry on, a strong arm to support us, we can go on. The sweetness found in sharing will sustain us, carry us, and give us hope.

But what if the bitterness arises within the very relationship from which we have been drawing our needed sweetness and strength? "It was not an enemy who reproached me, otherwise I could have borne it. Nor was it he who hated me that rose up against me, or I would have hid myself from him." But when it is that trusted and most intimate companion! The Apostle has said, "For those who love God, all things work together unto good" (Rom. 8:28). How can good come out of this?

Such things happen, for we are all poor, weak sinners, totally dependent on the Lord for light and strength, loyalty and love. It is perhaps only when all our human support fails, including that on which we most depended—whether it be by betrayal, divorce, or death—that we most need to hear the admonition, "Cast your burden upon the Lord, and he shall sustain you. He shall never allows a good person to be overcome." When all the created props, even the most precious one of loving friendship, of life-long partnership, are knocked out, then we open to hear and accept the ultimate truth of the Lord's word: "Without me you can do nothing" (John 15:5). When we have really been through it, when we have hit bottom, then we truly pray, "I will trust in you." Indeed we can trust the Lord, for he knows by experience the intense bitterness of being betrayed by an intimate friend: "Do you betray the Son of Man with a kiss?" (Luke 22:48). Suddenly all of the intimacy that we enjoyed through the years seems to have been a show. All the hopes and plans are shattered, all that we were going to do together dissolves. Death seems almost a merciful preference to living on with this wounding.

Before we get to this point, we are still apt to say, "Oh, that I had wings like a dove! For then would I fly away and be at rest." Happily would we escape all this suffering and anguish. We would have the serenity of the dove, cooing peacefully in the morning. But that would not be the way to true peace, to ultimate victory. We must stay and face the battle. But our artist hints at something. We do have wings, the wings of our guardian angel who is with us in the battle. So "I will call upon God and the Lord shall save me. Evening and morning and at noon I will pray and cry aloud and God shall hear my voice. God will give my soul peace, delivered from the battle.... "

Yes, my God , "I will trust in you."

Cry Out to God

Psalm 66

1 Cry out to God, all the earth!
2 Sing to the honor of God's name;
   give God glorious praise.
3 Say to God, "How awesome are your works!
   Because of the greatness of your power your enemies shall
      submit to you.
4 All the earth shall worship you and shall sing your praise;
   they shall sing in praise of your name."
5 Come and see the works of God;
   God is awesome in action among the people.
6 God turned the sea into dry land, they went through the
      waters on foot;
   let us rejoice in the Lord.
7 God rules forever by power, God's eyes keep watch on
      the nations;
   let not rebels rise up against the Lord.
8 Bless our God, you peoples; make the sound of God's
      praise heard,
9 God who gives us life and does not allow our feet to slip.
10 You, O God, have tested us;
   you have tried us as silver is tried.

11 You led us into the snare;
   you laid affliction upon our backs.
12 You have let people ride over us.
   We went through fire and through water,
   but you brought us out into a place of plenty.
13 I will enter your house with burnt offerings;
   I will pay to you my vows,
14 the vows which my lips have uttered
   and my mouth has spoken when I was in trouble.
15 I will offer to you burnt sacrifices of fatlings with the scent
      of burning rams;
   I will offer bullocks and goats.
16 Come and hear, all you who fear God,
   and I will tell you what he has done for my soul.
17 I cried to him with full voice
   and his praise was on my lips.
18 If I had cherished iniquity in my heart,
   the Lord would not have heard me.
19 But truly God has heard me;
   God has given heed to the voice of my prayer.
20 Blessed be God, who has not rejected my prayer
   nor deprived me of the divine mercy!

We went through fire and through water,
but you brought us out into a place of plenty.

Cry Out to God

Life is a journey—a journey to the Promised Land, to a place of unending joy. As we journey along, sometimes we are burned. More often we are flooded by cares and fears, overcome by tears of sorrow and desperation. It is all part of the journey unto life eternal.

We may question the fire and the water. Where is the love and loving care of the Lord? The Psalm tells us, "You, O God, test us; you try us as silver is tried." If we seem at times trapped in the snares of this life, if life's burdens seem to weigh heavily on our backs, if others seem to side against us, it is all a testing. Does this mean that God is the author of all that afflicts us? By no means! It does tell us a number of things: it tells us something of the power and might of our God. God is able to create men and women like unto God, with full freedom. God is able to fully respect the freedom God gives us even if it means we use our freedom to bring about great evil. It tells us God is able to use even the evil that comes from human malice to bring about good for those who love God. Testing purifies. Testing strengthens. Testing leads us through to victory and gives us cause for great joy. The Psalmist teaches us that through it all we should bless our God, "make the sound of God's praise heard," because through it all "God who gives us life does not allow our feet to slip." God hears us. God gives heed to the voice of our prayer. God never rejects us, never deprives us of the divine mercy. We will see what God has done, how "God is awesome in action among the people."

The Psalmist again calls forth from our memory the great moment of liberation. All seemed lost as the hordes of Pharaoh pressed down upon God's People. Then the wonder: God formed a dry path through the sea. But God's care didn't end there. There were vicissitudes a-many before the People passed through the waters of the Jordan and were brought "into a place of plenty." So will God enable us to pass through the waters of affliction—whatever they be and wherever they be. We will know that the Lord, who by his might worked the mighty deeds of the past, remains with us to teach us not only his power and might, wondrous though these may be. Through repeated and assiduous meditation of the Psalms, the Spirit will also teach us to look more deeply and, with ever greater insight and continued awareness, we will come to appreciate more fully the wonders of God's daily care.

As we become more and more fully aware of the God working in and through all, how God constantly "gives us life and does not allow our feet to slip," then the wondrous attitude of grateful praise spontaneously erupts from the depths of our being. We will call upon all the earth, the whole of creation, to help us to "give God glorious praise."

"All the earth shall worship you and shall sing your praise; they shall sing in praise of your name."

"Cry out to God, all the earth! Sing to the honor of God's name; give God glorious praise. Say to God, 'How awesome are your works!'"

In You, O Lord, I Place My Trust

Psalm 71

1 In you, O Lord, I place my trust; let me never be put
   to shame.
2 In your fidelity deliver me, grant that I might escape;
   listen to me and save me.
3 Be my strong dwelling place, where I may continually
   find refuge;
   give the command to save me, for you are my rock and
   my fortress.
4 Deliver me, my God, out of the hand of the wicked,
   out of the hand of the unjust and cruel.
5 For you are my hope, O Lord; in you have I trusted from
   my youth.
6 By you I have been supported from my birth;
   you are the one who took me from my mother's womb.
   I shall praise you without ceasing.
7 I am an enigma for many but you are my strong refuge.
8 My mouth is filled with your praise and with your glory all
   the day.

9 Cast me not off in my old age; forsake me not when my
    strength fails.
10 For my enemies speak against me
  and they that lie in wait for my soul take counsel together:
11 "God has forsaken him; pursue him and take him
  for there is no one to deliver him."
12 O God, be not far from me; O my God, make haste to
    help me.
13 Let my adversaries be put to shame;
  let them be covered with scorn and disgrace, those who
    seek my ruin.
14 But as for me, I will hope continually
  and will praise you more and more.
15 My mouth shall proclaim your righteousness and your
    saving deeds all the day,
  though they are beyond anything I can number.
16 I will declare the might of the Lord;
  I will proclaim your righteousness, yours alone.
17 O God, you have taught me from my youth
  and I am still proclaiming your wondrous works.
18 Now that I am old and gray-headed, O God, do not
    forsake me,
  so that I may declare your deliverance to all generations
    to come.
19 Your righteousness, O God, reaches to the heavens;
  you have done great things.
  O God, who is like unto you!
20 You have shown me great and sore troubles but you bring
    me back to life
  and bring me up again from the depths of the earth.

21 You increase my greatness and comfort me on every side.
22 I will praise you with the harp, my God, for
    your faithfulness;
  to you I will sing with the lyre, O Holy One of Israel.
23 My lips resound with joy when I sing to you
  for you have redeemed my soul.
24 My tongue proclaims your righteousness all the day long;
  for they are confounded, they are brought to shame, those
    who seek my hurt.

Cast me not off in my old age;
forsake me not when my strength fails.

In You, O Lord, I Place My Trust

his is the prayer of a content old person. Life has had its ups and downs: "By you I have been supported from my birth; you are the one who took me from my mother's womb.… You are my strong refuge." "O God, you have taught me from my youth.… You increase my greatness and comfort me on every side." And yet even now "enemies speak against me, and they that lie in wait for my soul take counsel together.… You have shown me great and sore troubles but you bring me back to life and bring me up again from the depths of the earth." So what is this elder's response? To pray with confidence and to praise: "My mouth shall proclaim your righteousness and your saving deeds all the day, though they are beyond anything I can number. I will declare the might of the Lord; I will proclaim your righteousness, yours alone."

Only one of the ten basic commands of the Lord is endowed with a promise: "Honor your father and your mother that your days may be long in the land which the Lord, your God, will give you" (Exod. 20:12). When the years no longer creep up on us but overtake us, we do indeed turn to the Lord and ask to be sustained in our old age as we struggle to sanctify our diminishments.

The Lord usually answers this prayer by bringing into our lives loving and caring family, friends and neighbors, companions for the journey. One of the truly beautiful stories of the Hebrew Bible is the story of Ruth. A young foreigner, a widow and childless, she was willing to go into exile to care for her equally bereaved mother-in-law, Naomi. There she undertook the painful and humiliating labor of the poor, that of a gleaner in the fields of others, in order to sustain their impoverished lives. The Lord rewarded her supremely. Her goodness touched the heart of the owner of the fields and soon she was taken as his wife. But that was not all. For she was to become the great-grandmother of King David and thus one of the mothers of the Messiah. Ruth's humble labors in the fields won her not only sustenance for herself and Naomi, but also a husband, Boaz, who was to father a royal line.

I do not know how I prayed this Psalm when I was young, but now that my strength is failing, it is most meaningful. I have trusted the Lord since my youth: "O God, you have taught me from my youth and I am still proclaiming your wondrous works." The Lord has been the constant theme of my praise. It is true—as my life unfolded, to many I seemed an enigma. The Lord has let me see "great and sore troubles." But he has indeed brought me back to life and brought me up again from the depths. With all my heart I make my own the words of the Psalmist:

> But as for me, I will hope continually
>   and will praise you more and more.
> My mouth shall proclaim your righteousness and your
>   saving deeds all the day,
> though they are beyond anything I can number.
> I will declare the might of the Lord;
> I will proclaim your righteousness, yours alone.

In you, O Lord, I place my trust. You are my rock and my fortress. Now that I am old and gray-headed, do not forsake me, so that I may declare to all generations to come your fidelity, your righteousness, your goodness that reaches to the very heavens.

This Psalm gives me the words I need to give some voice to the deepest sentiments of my heart. "You have done great things. O God, who is like unto you!"

Hear My Teaching

Psalm 78

1 Hear my teaching, my people. Turn your ears to the words
   of my mouth.

2 I will open my mouth in a parable. I will utter riddles
   of old.

3 What we have heard and known and our fathers have
   told us,

4 we will not hide from their children,
   telling the generation to come the praises of the Lord,
   his strength and the wonders the Lord has done.

5 For God established a Decree in Jacob and promulgated a
   Law in Israel,
   which God commanded our fathers
   that they should make known to their children,

6 so that the generation to come might know,
   the children yet unborn might arise and tell their children,

7 that they might set their hope in God and not forget the
   works of God
   but keep the commandments

8 and not be as their fathers, a stubborn and
    rebellious generation,
  a generation that was not loyal, whose spirit was not
    faithful to God.
9 The children of Ephraim, being armed and carrying bows,
    turned back in the day of battle.
10 They didn't keep God's covenant and refused to walk in
    God's law.
11 They forgot God's doings, the wondrous works that God
    had shown them.
12 God did marvelous things in the sight of their fathers,
  in the land of Egypt, in the plain of Zoan.
13 God split the sea and brought them through;
  God made the waters stand as a wall.
14 In the daytime God led them with a cloud
  and all night with a light of fire.
15 God split the rock in the wilderness
  and gave them to drink abundantly as out of the depths.
16 God brought streams out of the rock
  and caused waters to run down like rivers.
17 Yet they still went on sinning against God,
  rebelling against the Most High in the desert.
18 They tested God in their heart by demanding
    food according to their desires.
19 Yes, they spoke against God.
  They said, "Can God prepare a table in the wilderness?
20 Behold, God struck the rock, so that waters gushed out,
    streams flowed forth.
  Can God also give bread? Will God provide meat for
    the people?"

21 When Yahweh heard, there was anger;
   God's fire blazed against Jacob, God's anger rose
      against Israel,
22 because they had no faith in God and didn't trust in God's
      saving help.
23 Yet God commanded the skies above and opened the doors
      of heaven;
24 God rained down manna on them to eat and gave them
      food from the heavens.
25 Mortals ate the bread of angels; the Most High sent them
      food to the full.
26 God caused the east wind to blow across the sky;
   by divine power God sent forth the south wind.
27 God rained flesh on them like dust, winged birds as the
      sand on the seashore;
28 the birds fell in the midst of their camp, all around
      their tents.
29 So they ate and were filled; God gave them what
      they desired.
30 They hadn't satisfied their appetites; their food was yet in
      their mouths,
31 when the anger of God rose up against them.
   God killed some of the fittest among them,
   the Almighty struck down the young men of Israel.
32 In spite of all this they still sinned and didn't believe in
      God's wondrous works.
33 God let their days vanish like mist and their years like
      a phantom.
34 Whenever they were laid low, then they sought after God;
   they repented and sought God in earnest.

35 They remembered that God was their rock, the Most High
   their redeemer.
36 They flattered God with their mouth and lied to the Lord
   with their tongue,
37 for their heart was not right with God,
   they were not faithful to the divine covenant.
38 But being merciful, God forgave their iniquity
   and didn't destroy them.
   Yes, many times God restrained the divine anger
   and didn't stir up the divine wrath.
39 God remembered that they were but flesh,
   a breath that passes away and does not come again.

God split the sea and brought them through;
God made the waters stand as a wall.
In the daytime God led them with a cloud
and all night with a light of fire.

Hear My Teaching

*A*gain and again the Psalms rehearse the key events of the liberation of the Chosen People from their enslavement in Egypt. Even if these events are not actual history, as we would understand history today, but are rather mythological, they nonetheless invite the People of both Covenants to be mindful of God's most provident care and saving grace. This is why we listen, why we pray, meditate on, and sing the Psalms: to abide in mindfulness of God and the abundant mercy expressed in our lives in so many and such diverse ways.

Psalm 78 is one of the longer Psalms in the collection as it recounts the great events of liberation: "We will not hide them from their children, telling the generation to come the praises of the Lord, his strength and the wonders the Lord has done." The first great thing the inspired Psalmist brings forth is the gift of the Law, Torah, the Revelation, God's personal guidance. "For God established a Decree in Jacob and promulgated a Law in Israel." It was a gift that was to be passed on from generation to generation. Rabbi Jesus made it clear that he had come not to abolish the Law but to fulfill it (Matt. 5:17). It was to remain for us all a message from God that grounds our whole relationship with God. All else is an expression of this special Law and care, from the great initiating event of passing through the sea, something we experience in the New Covenant in our passage through the waters of Baptism. The Lord himself led them through the sea and continued to lead them day and night, in cloud and fire. And the Lord continues to lead us if we "set our hope in God and not forget the works of God and keep the commandments." The waters may seem to be piled high and very menacing. The journey may often seem to be in a cloud of unknowing or a dark night, but it is always sure, if we are but willing to listen and to follow.

Like our spiritual fathers and mothers in the desert journey, in spite of our repeated failures, our sins, our ungratefulness, as we journey toward our Promised Land, the Lord makes ever available to us the Bread of Heaven and the ever-flowing waters of divine grace. We suffer the consequences of our sins. God's justice and wisdom allow this so that we learn and become responsible and responsive People. God does not shield us like infants. For each of us God has worked wonders like unto all God did to liberate our spiritual ancestors, the Chosen People, from their enslavement. God has revealed to us the way to true freedom. If we continue to follow our own lights and reject God's lead, we will be punished and experience the consequences of our folly until we turn back like the prodigals that we are.

Our God is an amazing God. In our arrogance we dare to challenge God; in the face of all he has done and is doing for us, we dare to question his power and his goodness. In our times of great need, we cry out to God, but even then our hearts are not right with God. We still want our own way. We do not really believe and embrace God's covenant of love. But God, being a merciful God, does not destroy us. God restrains his righteous anger and stands ever ready to forgive.

God has established a People and given us a faithful leadership armed with the staff of the cross. With unselfish and unfailing care God leads us so that we "might set our hope in God and not forget the works of God but keep the commandments," and find our way safely to the Promised Land. This is the Good News we must not hide from our children but effectively make it known so that it can be passed from generation to generation, ever a source of hope even when the waters of tribulation seem to menacingly rise on every side. We have a God of liberation. No matter how much we fail our God, our God will never fail us.

You Who Dwell

Psalm 91

1 You who dwell in the shelter of the Most High,
    who abide under the shadow of the Almighty,
2 will say of the Lord, "My refuge and my fortress,
    my God, in whom I trust."
3 Surely the Lord will deliver you from the snare of
      the fowler
    and from the deadly pestilence.
4 The Divine will cover you with pinions,
    under the divine wings you will find refuge;
    God's fidelity shall be your buckler and shield.
5 You will not fear the terror by night,
    nor the arrow that flies by day,
6 nor the pestilence that goes about in the dark,
    nor the scourge that lays waste at noonday.
7 A thousand may fall at your left and ten thousand at
      your right
    but it will not come near you.
8 You have only to look, your eyes will see the reward of
      the wicked.
9 Because you have made the Lord your refuge,
    the Most High, your dwelling place,

10 therefore no evil shall befall you,
   no plague come near your tent.

· 11 For God will give angels charge over you to keep you in all
   your ways.

12 They will bear you in their hands, lest you dash your foot
   against a stone.

13 You will tread upon the lion and adder,
   the young lion and the serpent shall you
      trample underfoot.

14 "Those who love me, I will deliver;
   I will set them on high, those who acknowledge my name.

15 They will call upon me and I will answer them;
   I will be with them in trouble, I will deliver them
      and honor them.

16 With long life I will satisfy them and show them
   my salvation."

*The Divine will cover you with pinions,
under the divine wings you will find refuge.*

You Who Dwell

Night comes on. We seek to chase it away with our artificial light. We fill the hours with distractions: television, revelry, whatever we can. But deep within our human psyche we know the terrors of the night when darkness conquers light. The sun sets and a fickle moon casts only an eerie light. The stars are so far away.

Those of faith know where they can find refuge: under God's wings, under the wings of the Savior who has said he longs to gather us as little ones into his protection as a mother hen gathers her chicks beneath her wings (Matt. 23:37).

Each evening, as darkness begins to take hold, we can take up Psalm 91. We "who dwell in the shelter of the Most High, who abide under the shadow of the Almighty, will say of the Lord, 'My refuge and my fortress, my God, in whom I trust.'" He will deliver us from every evil. We "will not be afraid of the terror by night … nor of the pestilence that goes about in the dark." This confidence will abide with us. It will spill over into the day. We will not fear "the arrow that flies by day … nor the scourge that lays waste at noonday," for the same divine protection will still be with us. Winged angels, are they not the "pinions" of the Lord? "God will give angels charge over you to keep you in all your ways. They will bear you in their hands, lest you dash your foot against a stone."

I do not think we appreciate enough the loving care of these fellow creatures, so superior to us yet commissioned to serve us and care for us. Remember the wonderful story of Raphael, sent to care for Tobit? Powerful and all embracing is their care. No matter what form the threats take on — be they ferocious and savage like those of the mighty lion; or as insidious as the poison of the adder; or a deadly pestilence like AIDS or SARS; or the threats of muggers and street gangs — we will not fear. For we have heard these words of the Most High, the All-Powerful, uttered through the inspired Psalmist: "Those who love me, I will deliver; I will set them on high, those who acknowledge my name. They will call upon me and I will answer them; I will be with them in trouble, I will deliver them and honor them. With long life I will satisfy them and show them my salvation."

How better can we as individuals or families enter into the night and find peace—the restful, restorative peace that is hidden therein—than by letting the Word of the Lord, this Psalm of divine reassurance, again speak to us? This is the evening prayer that the Lord himself has given us. It leads us to pray with confidence, "My refuge and my fortress; my God, in whom I trust." We are not alone when we pray it. Through the centuries, men of prayer have donned their prayer shawls and murmured these consoling and comforting words; monks and nuns and other communities of the faithful all around the globe end their day with this good Word. We can join this immense human choir as we watch the light of the sun fade, the evening star arise, and the moon begin to give its light. We can sense the great motherly wings of God hovering over us and drawing us into the warmth of their loving care, we who dwell in the shelter of the Most High and abide under the shadow of the Almighty.

The Lord Reigns

Psalm 97

1 The Lord reigns, let the earth rejoice!
Let the many islands be glad!
2 Clouds and darkness are round about the Lord;
righteousness and judgment are the foundation of
God's throne.
3 A fire goes before the Lord and burns up enemies on
every side.
4 The Lord's lightning bolts light up the world,
the earth sees and trembles.
5 The hills melt like wax at the presence of the Lord,
at the presence of the Lord of the whole earth.
6 The heavens proclaim the Lord's goodness
and all the people see God's glory.
7 Confounded be all who serve graven images,
who boast of their idols.
Worship the Lord, all you gods!
8 Zion hears and is glad,
the daughters of Judah rejoice because of your judgments,
O Lord.
9 For you, Lord, are high above all the earth;
you are exalted far above all gods.

10 The Lord loves those who hate evil.
   Preserves the life of his saints;
   the Lord delivers them out of the hand of the wicked.
11 Light is sown for the good
   and joy for the upright in heart.
12 Rejoice in the Lord, you just ones,
   and give thanks to the Lord's holy Name.

Light is sown for the good
and joy for the upright in heart.

The Lord Reigns

What is it going to be like when "the Lord of the whole earth" comes? The Lord is King; the heavens proclaim God's goodness. For us "cloud and darkness are round about the Lord." We know so little, the creation seems so opaque—a cloud of unknowing; a dark, dark night. We know goodness and justice are God's prerogatives. We have seen shadows of God's awesomeness in the creation: "God's lightning bolts light up the world." Earth quakes, mountains melt, and lands are washed away. How much more would we see?

When the true People of God hear of God's coming there will be exaltation and joy. We will not fear God's greatness, for we know the Lord guards the life of the devout, of those who turn against evil. For God's People, those who have chosen the path of virtue, God's coming will bring light—no longer will clouds and darkness surround him. God's lightnings will light up the world. For those who worship created things and take pride — in the idols they themselves have made—wealth, prestige, power it will be a devouring fire. But for God's virtuous ones it will reveal the divine glory. It will be a Taboric light that will embrace them, and, even as it overawes them, will bring the assuring revelation of a heavenly Father's love, of the fulfillment of the Law of Moses and the prophecies of Elijah. Light will be sown for the good and joy for the upright in heart.

This is the wonder that is promised us. So even now, remembering his faithfulness, we can rejoice in the Lord. We have much cause for joy. It is time to praise him.

Rightly then does our artist offer us not one but two, not ten-stringed but eleven-stringed harps, caught up in the whole exciting movement of chaotic celebration. Hands, male and female, reach out, wide open to the light, the light sown for the good. It is all a wild dance, striving to express the inexpressible, the joy that the experience of the divine light will evoke in us. We want to grasp the harps and play. We want to reach out and make the light our own. But well we know, grasping only closes the hand in darkness. An openness, a wide-open spirit alone can welcome the light that is sown in us and let it give birth to the inexpressible. The truly upright heart, the pure heart, will come to see God and become worthy to be a child of God.

The Lord reigns; indeed God does. And all God's judgments are just. The People of God are glad. We have much cause for rejoicing—the whole earth, every bit of land that rises from out of the seas. For the Lord, everything is solidly founded on goodness and justice. All shall see God's glory.

"Rejoice in the Lord, you just ones, and give thanks to the Lord's holy Name."

Sing to the Lord

Psalm 98

1 Sing to the Lord a new song, for God has done
 marvelous things!
 The Lord's right hand and the Lord's holy arm have
 brought the victory.
2 The Lord has made known saving power,
 God has revealed saving power to the nations.
3 God has been mindful of mercy and fidelity toward the
 house of Israel.
 All the ends of the earth have seen the saving power of
 our God.
4 Sing to the Lord with joy, all the earth!
 Burst into song and rejoice and sing praise!
5 Sing to the Lord with the harp, with the harp and a voice
 that delights.
6 With trumpets and the horn make a joyful noise before
 the Lord, the King!

7 Let the sea roar and all that fills it, the world and all who
   dwell there.
8 Let the rivers clap their hands, let the hills sing together
   for joy
9 at the presence of the Lord when the Lord comes to rule
   the earth.
   With saving power the Lord will govern the world and rule
   the people with equity.

Sing to the Lord with the harp....
With trumpets and the horn....

Sing to the Lord

*T*he Lord has made known saving power, has revealed saving power to the nations. God has done marvelous things.

The Psalmist is a man of faith, of intuition, of presence. Even when these marvels are worked through the forces of nature, even when men and women are the agents of God's saving power, he perceives it is the Lord at work: "The Lord's right hand and the Lord's holy arm have brought the victory." All the ends of the earth have seen the saving power of our God. And more. The Psalmist perceives that the Lord is present to "govern the world and rule the people with equity."

Sharing in his perceptions we join in his cry, his prayer of praise. As high priests of creation we call upon the thundering seas and all that is within them, the rivers that feed them, and even the mountain sources, to join in a chorus of joy. More, we add to the voice of our own praise that of our hands, the heavenly sounds of the harps. And still yet more is wanted. We call upon trumpets and horns and many other instruments to join with us as we acclaim the Lord as the true King of the Creation. There is never enough celebration of this all good and infinitely merciful God, the source of all good.

We know that all that is, is God's gift and it is a constant and unfailing gift. Mindful of God's mercy and fidelity we want to sing to the Lord an ever-new song, an unending song. Yes, we want to sing the age-old songs of the Psalter, but we want to sing them with a newness and a freshness, with an exuberance and a joy, with an appreciation and gratitude that makes them wholly new, unlike they have ever sounded before. A song is a song when it is sung. We want to give new being to the Psalms and each Psalm in its turn.

Within this experience there are ecstatic moments. How wonderful are the moments when we close our eyes and, as it were, go beyond. Better yet if our well-trained fingers can play the strings of the harp and give expression to the deepest sentiments of our soul. Perhaps no instrument is so gentle and so able to be attuned to the movements of the heart. And yet there is a part of us that says this is not enough. There are parts of us that would want to shout and praise God, but rather let trumpets and horns give voice—louder, stronger, more forcefully, more fully, while they yet leave the depths of our being in its quiet ecstasy. Our whole being, every fiber of it, reaches, stretches, strains, aches to be close to God. Can anything satisfy the one who has come to know the Lord through the creation and the re-creation, through God's marvelous deeds, the triumphs God has wrought for the People God calls his own?

All that rises from the depths of our being must come to know the Lord's mercy—something we can come to know only from the depths of our own sinfulness and misery—and the Lord's fidelity—something we know only in the face of our countless and continuous failures. The Lord's saving mercy reaches from one end of the earth to the other. Everyone and everything speaks to us of it by their very being. Everything calls forth from us the imperative: "Sing to the Lord a new song."

Hear My Prayer

Psalm 102

1 Hear my prayer, O Lord; let my cry come to you.

2 Do not turn your face from me when I am in distress.
   Incline your ear to me when I call, hasten to answer me.

3 For my days disappear like smoke; my bones burn like
   glowing embers.

4 My heart is scorched and withered like grass; I am
   consumed by the devourer.

5 I am exhausted by my loud groaning; I am reduced to skin
   and bones.

6 I am like a bird in the wilderness, like an owl in
   desolate places.

7 I am unable to sleep; I have become like a bird alone on
   a roof.

8 All day long my enemies taunt me; those who mock me
   defile my name.

9 Ashes are my food; tears, my drink.

10 Because of your fury and wrath, you have taken me up and
   thrown me down.

11 My days are like a fading shadow and I wither like grass.

12 But you, O Lord, sit enthroned forever;
   your throne endures from age to age.

13 Rise up and have pity on Zion, for it is time to show pity;
  the time has come.
14 Your servants love her stones;
  her very dust moves them to pity.
15 The nations revere your name, O Lord;
  all the kings of the earth, your glory.
16 For the Lord rebuilds Zion and appears in glory.
17 The Lord will respond to the prayer of the destitute;
  the Lord will not despise their plea.
18 Let this be written for the next generation,
  that a people yet to be born may praise the Lord:
19 "The Lord looked down from his sanctuary on high,
  from heaven the Lord looked upon the earth,
20 to hear the groans of the prisoners
  and to release those condemned to die.
21 So the name of the Lord will be proclaimed in Zion
  and his praise in Jerusalem
22 when the peoples and the kings of the earth gather to serve
    the Lord."
23 The Lord has shattered my strength; the Lord has cut short
    my days.
24 "Do not take me away before I have lived half my days
  while your years go on through generations.
25 Long ago you laid the foundations of the earth
  and the heavens are your handiwork.
26 They will perish but you will remain; all of them will wear
    out like clothes.
  You change them like a garment and they pass away.
27 But you remain the same,
  and your years will never end.
28 The children of your servants will live in your presence;
  their descendants will be before you forever."

*My days are like a fading shadow
and I wither like grass.*

Hear My Prayer

"The span of our life is seventy years—eighty for those who are strong" (Ps. 90:10). I have trod this earth three score and ten plus a few. I do not know if I am among the strong. My days are like a fading shadow and I wither like grass. I do not know the day or the hour, but I have full confidence that the Lord will complete the work that God wants to do in and through my life, and then take me home.

I do not know how any one can ever be bored. The days pass so quickly. They vanish and there is always so much more to do. I can hardly find the time I want to enjoy these wonderful songs, to drink in their wisdom, to let them open my mind and my heart.

I am withering like grass. I seek to sanctify my diminishments. Sometimes it is a struggle. I seem to have to give more and more time and attention to the care of this aging body: trips to the doctors and specialists and the hospital and labs; medications, therapies and exercise programs; and just plain eating. Even that seems to take longer and consume more time. "Ashes are my food; tears, my drink." I wither and time vanishes.

But ... But I move toward the great light. If anything shadows my life it is the light of what truly is and will be.

Hear my prayer, O Lord; let my cry come to you. Do not turn your face from me when I am in distress. Incline your ear to me when I call, hasten to answer me.

Although my days disappear like smoke and I know aches and pains, loneliness, and even mockery, I do not fear. I do not give up hope. Indeed, I am full of confidence. For you rise up and have pity on Zion. You will appear in glory and will respond to the prayer of the destitute. You will not despise my plea.

It is time to think of what heritage I am to leave. Let this be written for the next generation, that a people yet to be born may praise the Lord and his praise sound forth when the peoples and the kings of the earth gather to serve the Lord. Let this be my consolation: you remain the same and your years will never end. The children of your servants will live in your presence; their descendants will be before you forever.

My days are numbered. I shall soon pass to join my fathers and mothers. Even the heavens and the earth will pass away. God's handiwork through the ages will perish but the Lord will remain the same. God's years will never end. There'll be a new heaven and a new earth. And we shall all live on in the joy of the Lord for ever.

The Lord does indeed turn his face to me; he does incline his ear to me. The Lord has looked down from his sanctuary on high and has filled my heart with hope. My days may vanish, I may indeed wither, but this is only the prelude to passing from this limited life to that domain where I will be in the presence of the Lord forever.

Give Thanks to the Lord

Psalm 136

1 Give thanks to the Lord, for the Lord is good,
the Lord's mercy endures for ever.

2 Give thanks to the God of gods,
for God's mercy endures for ever.

3 Give thanks to the Lord of lords,
for Lord's mercy endures for ever;

4 to the Lord who alone does great wonders,
for the Lord's mercy endures for ever;

5 to the Lord who by wisdom made the heavens,
for the Lord's mercy endures for ever;

6 to the Lord that stretched out the earth above the waters,
for the Lord's mercy endures for ever;

7 to the Lord who made the great lights,
for the Lord's mercy endures for ever;

8 the sun to rule the day,
for the Lord's mercy endures for ever;

9 the moon and stars to rule the night,
for the Lord's mercy endures for ever;

10 to the Lord who smote Egypt in their firstborn,
for the Lord's mercy endures for ever;

11 and brought out Israel from among them,
for the Lord's mercy endures for ever;

12 with a strong hand and with an outstretched arm,
    for the Lord's mercy endures for ever;
13 to the Lord who divided the Red Sea,
    for the Lord's mercy endures for ever;
14 and made Israel to pass through it,
    for the Lord's mercy endures for ever;
15 but overthrew Pharaoh and his host in the Red Sea,
    for the Lord's mercy endures for ever;
16 to the Lord who led the Lord's people through
        the wilderness,
    for the Lord's mercy endures for ever;
17 to the Lord who smote great kings,
    for the Lord's mercy endures for ever;
18 and slew famous kings,
    for the Lord's mercy endures for ever;
19 Sihon king of the Amorites,
    for the Lord's mercy endures for ever;
20 and Og the king of Bashan,
    for the Lord's mercy endures for ever;
21 and gave their land as a heritage,
    for the Lord's mercy endures for ever;
22 a heritage to Israel, the Lord's servant,
    for the Lord's mercy endures for ever;
23 who remembered us in our lowliness,
    for the Lord's mercy endures for ever;
24 and redeemed us from our enemies,
    for the Lord's mercy endures for ever;
25 who gives food to all,
    for the Lord's mercy endures for ever.
26 O give thanks to the God of heaven,
    for God's mercy endures for ever!

The sun to rule the day ...
the moon and stars to rule the night.

Give Thanks to the Lord

I look out upon the creation. The sun is rising (though in truth it is our little world that has spun around) and all is lit up—a glorious dawn, with gentle hues from deepest purple to true gold, heralding in the coming of the day star. Rising, the sun asserts its majesty and all the lesser lights are lost in its all embracing light.

The moon was very full last night (in truth, it stood just opposite the hidden sun and reflected for us the sun's light as fully as it could). We could walk without fear, as it shone on our path. So bright it hid many of the stars, though they are in fact so much more powerful. A shyer moon that shows but a sliver of its reflected light has allowed us on other nights to gaze with amazement on the whole carpet of stars, points of light beyond counting, blinking through countless miles of space years, coming to delight us now.

O give thanks to the God of gods ... to the Lord of lords ... for the Lord is good! The Lord alone does such great wonders ... the Lord alone makes the heavens. God's Law endures forever.

Great and awesome is God's might and power, and wondrous the great works of God's creation, yet God reaches down with mighty and tender care. God cares for us. We do not need to fear any foe, no matter how mighty, for God's steadfast love endures forever. God is profoundly aware of our low estate. And as long as we are aware of it and open to humbly receive help, God will rescue us from all our foes. God will provide for all our needs in the ample provision of the creation. No one need hunger upon this earth if we would but effectively acknowledge that it is God's gift to us all, and share it accordingly. It is only our selfishness that leads to the hunger of many while we store provisions for tomorrow. We forget the lesson of the manna in the desert and how Jesus taught us to pray for "our daily bread." In the end our stores become a waste and burden after they have eroded our sense of thanksgiving, our appreciation of the steadfast love of the providing hand of our Provident Lord.

Give thanks to the Lord, for the Lord is good, the Lord's mercy endures for ever. Give thanks to the God of gods, for God's mercy endures for ever. Give thanks to the Lord of lords, for Lord's mercy endures for ever.

May the Lord give us a spirit of wisdom and a perception of what is revealed to us to bring us to full knowledge of the Lord. May God enlighten the eyes of our mind so that we can see what hope God's call holds for us. How rich is the glory of the heritage God offers his holy People. And how extraordinarily great is the power that God exercises for us (Eph. 1:17–19). The events of the Exodus may seem very remote to us now, even when we celebrate them and seek to relive them in the Paschal Mystery of the Passover, but God's wondrous creation is ever around us—yes, sun and moon and stars, planets and galaxies and the solid earth beneath our feet; the water that slakes our thirst and washes our faces; the food that nourishes us and gives us life. If we have any mindfulness, any spiritual awareness, we must cry out: The mercy of the Lord endures forever.

Beside the Rivers of Babylon

Psalm 137

1 Beside the rivers of Babylon,
   there we sat and wept when we remembered Zion;
2 there upon the willows we hung up our harps.
3 For those who had carried us away captive demanded a
      song of us,
   those who mocked us demanded songs of joy,
   "Sing us one of the songs of Zion!"
4 How shall we sing the Lord's song in a strange land?
5 If I forget you, Jerusalem, let my right hand lose all its skill.
6 If I do not remember you, let my tongue cleave to the roof
      of my mouth,
   if Jerusalem be not my chief joy.

7 Remember, Lord, the children of Edom in the day of
    Jerusalem's fall,
  those who said, "Raze it, raze it, even to its foundations!"
8 O daughters of Babylon, who are to be destroyed,
  a blessing on the one
  who repays you as you have paid us.
9 A blessing on the one
  who takes your little ones and dashes them against
    the stones.

Beside the rivers of Babylon,
there we sat and wept when we remembered Zion;
there upon the willows we hung up our harps.

Beside the Rivers of Babylon

I dare say most of us have at one time or another wished we could leave it all behind and go sit by a quietly flowing river and let our tears mingle with its clear, cool waters. Exiles—not because some evil force has carried us off physically but because the aches and pains, the sorrows and disappointments of life are alienating us from our surroundings. Certainly at such a time there was no desire to take up a harp or any other instrument and sing a song. Perhaps a dirge seemed more in order, tuning itself to the murmurings of the river.

In "Salve Regina," one of the much-loved and frequently sung hymns of the People of God, we sing of ourselves as "the exiled children of Eve." Some days more than others we are acutely aware that we are an exiled People, we live in a land of exile. The Promised Land lies ahead—a promise not yet realized: the true Zion, the land of unending life and joy and peace.

So for now, we sit in this our land of exile. And we have cause for weeping. Our exile is not so much geographical as, a state of being, caused by our sin. God's plan was a garden that opened out into Paradise. But our forebears chose to decide things for themselves. And the result was disaster. And we all suffer the consequences. But let us not be too hard on them. We all fail again and again, choosing our own ill-conceived plans rather than God's plan, which is the only sure way home.

We may not feel like taking up harps and singing the glorious Psalms of the Temple, but it is essential that we count the heavenly Jerusalem the greatest of our joys, that we never forget this Jerusalem but keep our eyes on this goal, our true home. If we feel like cursing, we may well call down a curse on the unmindfulness that causes us to fail to be constantly aware of this, allowing it to give meaning and color to our lives and all that we do.

When we look back upon our own personal journey as it has unfolded through the years, we may well want to call down a curse on some of those whom we sense have caused us to suffer in one way or another. But such bitterness, such cursing, only increases the bitterness of our exile. Ultimately, even though evil forces have worked against us, it is our own sin that causes us to be exiled from the deep peace and joy that can be ours even on the exile's journey. Happiness consists in knowing what we want and knowing we have it or are on the way to getting it. We are on the way. We have the sure help of God to get what we want, and even more: "Eye has not seen, ear has not heard, nor has it even entered into the human mind what God has prepared for those who love him … " (1 Cor. 2:10). Even this life in exile can be shot through with the joy of an evergreen hope.

So maybe it is time to take down our harps and sing songs of praise and joy made vibrant by a sure hope, "because of the faithful love of our God, in which the rising sun has come from on high to visit us and to give light to those who live in darkness and the shadow of death and to guide our feet in the ways of peace" (Luke 1:78–79).

Alleluia

Psalm 150

1 Alleluia!
Praise God in his holy place;
praise him in his exalted power!
2 Praise him for his mighty deeds;
praise him for his exceeding greatness!
3 Praise him with the sound of the trumpet;
praise him with the lyre and harp!
4 Praise him with tambourines and dance;
praise him with strings and pipes!
5 Praise him with clashing cymbals;
praise him with resounding cymbals!
6 Let everything that breathes praise the Lord!
Alleluia!

Let everything that breathes praise the Lord!

Alleluia

*J*oy! Joy! Joy!

Celebrate! How else could we conclude this wonderful collection of Psalms? Our whole being wants to celebrate. And still it is not enough. So we take up all the wonderful instruments that can magnify the voice of our praise.

It is undoubtedly fitting that this consecrated collection of songs should end with a final chorus of praise, a great doxology to close the Psalter.

If we have really let the Psalter form our minds and hearts, this is the only thing we can do at this point: be before God in praise.

Indeed, I wonder if we really know what praise means. Or how to praise. How can we come to be filled with the spirit of praise? This I think is the role of the Psalter, to teach us to praise.

We begin to learn to praise God in his temple on earth, joining with others, taking up the inspired hymns, allowing words, thoughts, concepts, feelings, images, colors, the whole lived experience of the Chosen People of God to draw us forth to the highest level of human being, which prepares us to praise God in God's temple in heaven.

Psalm after Psalm has recalled for us God's mighty achievements. We have rehearsed them and lived them again and again, as the Psalms rose from our daily prayer. And these were the doorways that opened to give us some slight perception of God's transcendent greatness.

Even a hint of this greatness calls us to a praise that is beyond us. With an almost chaotic fever, our fervor calls for all the instruments that we have been able to devise to magnify our sentiments and aspirations. We call upon lyre and harp, all the stringed instruments, and all the reeds, the blasting trumpets and clashing cymbals. It is not enough. It is not sufficient for us. We call upon all the beautiful and rhythmic movements of our own bodies. But still we want something more total, more intimate: the very breath of life and being that takes its source from deep within. We call upon not only all the breathing creation, human and animal; we would have "everything that breathes"—all, taken up in the Divine Breath. For we, in truth, do not know how to pray as we ought (Rom. 8:26), but Holy Spirit, the Breath of God, raises up within us a total and complete, "Alleluia! Praise God!"

This powerful, beautiful little doxology takes up all the praise of the Psalter, of the human heart, of the creation, and brings it into the very Trinity, where the Son, one with Holy Spirit, gives to the Father perfect praise in giving the totality of his divine being. Nothing less than this will suffice to adequately praise the awesome, immense, and indescribable goodness of the God who is the beneficent source of all that is, of all that we are.

Alleluia! Praise the Lord!

Suggested Reading

Bonhoeffer, Dietrich. *Psalms: The Prayer Book of the Bible*. Minneapolis: Augsburg Fortress, 1974.

Corcoran, Nancy. *Secrets of Prayer: A Multifaith Guide to Creating Personal Prayer in Your Life*. Woodstock, VT: SkyLight Paths, 2007.

Cummings, Charles. *Songs of Freedom: The Psalter as a School of Prayer*. Danville, NJ: Dimension, 1986.

Dahood, Mitchell. *Psalms, The Anchor Bible*. 3 vols. Garden City, NY: Doubleday, 1965–70.

John Paul, II (pope). *Psalms and Canticles: Meditations and Catechesis on the Psalms and Canticles of Morning Prayer*. Chicago: Liturgical Training Publications, 2004.

Lewis, C. S. *Reflections on the Psalms*. Fort Washington, PA: Harvest, 1964.

Mowinckel, Sigmund. *The Psalms in Israel's Worship*. Grand Rapids, MI: Eerdmans, 2004.

Oesterley, W. O. E. *The Psalms*. London: SPCK, 1962.

Pennington, M. Basil. *Finding Grace at the Center, 3rd Ed.: The Beginning of Centering Prayer*. Woodstock, VT: SkyLight Paths, 2007.

———. *The Monks of Mount Athos: A Western Monk's Extraordinary Spiritual Journey on Eastern Holy Ground*. Woodstock, VT: SkyLight Paths, 2003.

———. *Poetry as Prayer: The Psalms*. Boston: Pauline, 2001.

———. *The Song of Songs: A Spiritual Commentary*. Woodstock, VT: SkyLight Paths, 2007.

Polish, Daniel. *Bringing the Psalms to Life: How to Understand and Use the Book of Psalms*. Woodstock, VT: Jewish Lights, 2001.

———. *Keeping Faith with the Psalms: Deepen Your Relationship with God Using the Book of Psalms*. Woodstock, VT: Jewish Lights, 2005.

Stuhlmueller, Carroll. *Psalms 1: Old Testament Message*. Wilmington, DE: Michael Glazier, 1983.

———. *Psalms 2: Old Testament Message*. Wilmington, DE: Michael Glazier, 1983.

Weintraub, Simkha Y., ed. *Healing of Soul, Healing of Body: Spiritual Leaders Unfold the Strength and Solace in Psalms*. Woodstock, VT: Jewish Lights, 1994.

Global Spiritual Perspectives

Spiritual Perspectives on America's Role as Superpower
by the Editors at SkyLight Paths

Are we the world's good neighbor or a global bully? From a spiritual perspective, what are America's responsibilities as the only remaining superpower? Contributors: **Dr. Beatrice Bruteau • Dr. Joan Brown Campbell • Tony Campolo • Rev. Forrest Church • Lama Surya Das • Matthew Fox • Kabir Helminski • Thich Nhat Hanh • Eboo Patel • Abbot M. Basil Pennington, ocso • Dennis Prager • Rosemary Radford Ruether • Wayne Teasdale • Rev. William McD. Tully • Rabbi Arthur Waskow • John Wilson**

5½ x 8½, 256 pp, Quality PB, 978-1-893361-81-2 **$16.95**

Spiritual Perspectives on Globalization, 2nd Edition
Making Sense of Economic and Cultural Upheaval
by Ira Rifkin; Foreword by Dr. David Little, Harvard Divinity School

What is globalization? Surveys the religious landscape. Includes a new Discussion Guide designed for group use.

5½ x 8½, 256 pp, Quality PB, 978-1-59473-045-0 **$16.99**

Hinduism / Vedanta

The Four Yogas
A Guide to the Spiritual Paths of Action, Devotion, Meditation and Knowledge
 by Swami Adiswarananda
6 x 9, 320 pp, Quality PB, 978-1-59473-223-2 **$19.99**; HC, 978-1-59473-143-3 **$29.99**

Meditation & Its Practices
A Definitive Guide to Techniques and Traditions of Meditation in Yoga and Vedanta
by Swami Adiswarananda 6 x 9, 504 pp, Quality PB, 978-1-59473-105-1 **$24.99**

The Spiritual Quest and the Way of Yoga: The Goal, the Journey and the Milestones
by Swami Adiswarananda 6 x 9, 288 pp, HC, 978-1-59473-113-6 **$29.99**

Sri Ramakrishna, the Face of Silence
by Swami Nikhilananda and Dhan Gopal Mukerji
Edited with an Introduction by Swami Adiswarananda; Foreword by Dhan Gopal Mukerji II
Classic biographies present the life and thought of Sri Ramakrishna.
6 x 9, 352 pp, HC, 978-1-59473-115-0 **$29.99**

Sri Sarada Devi, The Holy Mother: Her Teachings and Conversations
Translated with Notes by Swami Nikhilananda; Edited with an Introduction by Swami Adiswarananda
6 x 9, 288 pp, HC, 978-1-59473-070-2 **$29.99**

The Vedanta Way to Peace and Happiness by Swami Adiswarananda
6 x 9, 240 pp, Quality PB, 978-1-59473-180-8 **$18.99**

Vivekananda, World Teacher: His Teachings on the Spiritual Unity of Humankind
Edited and with an Introduction by Swami Adiswarananda
6 x 9, 272 pp, Quality PB, 978-1-59473-210-2 **$21.99**

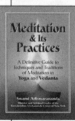

Sikhism

The First Sikh Spiritual Master
Timeless Wisdom from the Life and Teachings of Guru Nanak by Harish Dhillon
Tells the story of a unique spiritual leader who showed a gentle, peaceful path to God-realization while highlighting Guru Nanak's quest for tolerance and compassion. 6 x 9, 192 pp, Quality PB, 978-1-59473-209-6 **$16.99**

Or phone, fax, mail or e-mail to: SKYLIGHT PATHS Publishing
Sunset Farm Offices, Route 4 • P.O. Box 237 • Woodstock, Vermont 05091
Tel: (802) 457-4000 • Fax: (802) 457-4004 • www.skylightpaths.com
Credit card orders: (800) 962-4544 (8:30AM–5:30PM ET Monday–Friday)
Generous discounts on quantity orders. SATISFACTION GUARANTEED. Prices subject to change.

Judaism / Christianity / Interfaith

Talking about God: Exploring the Meaning of Religious Life with Kierkegaard, Buber, Tillich and Heschel *by Daniel F. Polish, PhD*
Examines the meaning of the human religious experience with the greatest theologians of modern times.   6 x 9, 176 pp, HC, 978-1-59473-230-0 **$21.99**

Interactive Faith: The Essential Interreligious Community-Building Handbook
Edited by Rev. Bud Heckman with Rori Picker Neiss
A guide to the key methods and resources of the interfaith movement.
6 x 9, 400 pp (est), HC, 978-1-59473-237-9 **$40.00**

The Jewish Approach to Repairing the World (*Tikkun Olam*)
A Brief Introduction for Christians   *by Rabbi Elliot N. Dorff, PhD*
A window into the Jewish idea of responsibility to care for the world.
5½ x 8½, 192 pp (est), Quality PB, 978-1-58023-349-1 **$16.99** (a Jewish Lights book)

Modern Jews Engage the New Testament: Enhancing Jewish Well-Being in a Christian Environment *by Rabbi Michael J. Cook, PhD*
A look at the dynamics of the New Testament.
6 x 9, 416 pp, HC, 978-1-58023-313-2 **$29.99** (a Jewish Lights book)

Disaster Spiritual Care: Practical Clergy Responses to Community, Regional and National Tragedy
Edited by Rabbi Stephen B. Roberts, BCJC, & Rev. Willard W.C. Ashley, Sr., DMin, DH
The definitive reference for pastoral caregivers of all faiths involved in disaster response.
6 x 9, 384 pp, Hardcover, 978-1-59473-240-9 **$40.00**

The Changing Christian World: A Brief Introduction for Jews
by Rabbi Leonard A. Schoolman
5½ x 8½, 176 pp, Quality PB, 978-1-58023-344-6 **$16.99** (a Jewish Lights book)

The Jewish Connection to Israel, the Promised Land: A Brief Introduction for Christians *by Rabbi Eugene Korn, PhD*
5½ x 8½, 192 pp, Quality PB, 978-1-58023-318-7 **$14.99** (a Jewish Lights book)

Christians and Jews in Dialogue: Learning in the Presence of the Other
by Mary C. Boys and Sara S. Lee; Foreword by Dorothy C. Bass
Inspires renewed commitment to dialogue between religious traditions.
6 x 9, 240 pp, HC, 978-1-59473-144-0 **$21.99**

Healing the Jewish-Christian Rift: Growing Beyond Our Wounded History
by Ron Miller and Laura Bernstein; Foreword by Dr. Beatrice Bruteau
6 x 9, 288 pp, Quality PB, 978-1-59473-139-6 **$18.99**

Introducing My Faith and My Community
The Jewish Outreach Institute Guide for the Christian in a Jewish Interfaith Relationship
by Rabbi Kerry M. Olitzky 6 x 9, 176 pp, Quality PB, 978-1-58023-192-3 **$16.99** *(a Jewish Lights book)*

The Jewish Approach to God: A Brief Introduction for Christians
by Rabbi Neil Gillman 5½ x 8½, 192 pp, Quality PB, 978-1-58023-190-9 **$16.95** *(a Jewish Lights book)*

Jewish Holidays: A Brief Introduction for Christians
by Rabbi Kerry M. Olitzky and Rabbi Daniel Judson
5½ x 8½, 176 pp, Quality PB, 978-1-58023-302-6 **$16.99** *(a Jewish Lights book)*

Jewish Ritual: A Brief Introduction for Christians
by Rabbi Kerry M. Olitzky and Rabbi Daniel Judson
5½ x 8½, 144 pp, Quality PB, 978-1-58023-210-4 **$14.99** *(a Jewish Lights book)*

Jewish Spirituality: A Brief Introduction for Christians *by Rabbi Lawrence Kushner*
5½ x 8½, 112 pp, Quality PB, 978-1-58023-150-3 **$12.95** *(a Jewish Lights book)*

A Jewish Understanding of the New Testament
by Rabbi Samuel Sandmel; new Preface by Rabbi David Sandmel
5½ x 8½, 368 pp, Quality PB, 978-1-59473-048-1 **$19.99**

We Jews and Jesus: Exploring Theological Differences for Mutual Understanding
by Rabbi Samuel Sandmel; new Preface by Rabbi David Sandmel A Classic Reprint
6 x 9, 192 pp, Quality PB, 978-1-59473-208-9 **$16.99**

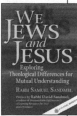

Show Me Your Way: The Complete Guide to Exploring Interfaith Spiritual Direction
by Howard A. Addison 5½ x 8½, 240 pp, Quality PB, 978-1-893361-41-6 **$16.95**

Midrash Fiction / Folktales

Abraham's Bind & Other Bible Tales of Trickery, Folly, Mercy and Love by Michael J. Caduto

New retellings of episodes in the lives of familiar biblical characters explore relevant life lessons.

6 x 9, 224 pp, HC, 978-1-59473-186-0 **$19.99**

Daughters of the Desert: Stories of Remarkable Women from Christian, Jewish and Muslim Traditions by Claire Rudolf Murphy, Meghan Nuttall

Sayres, Mary Cronk Farrell, Sarah Conover and Betsy Wharton

Breathes new life into the old tales of our female ancestors in faith. Uses traditional scriptural passages as starting points, then with vivid detail fills in historical context and place. Chapters reveal the voices of Sarah, Hagar, Huldah, Esther, Salome, Mary Magdalene, Lydia, Khadija, Fatima and many more. Historical fiction ideal for readers of all ages. Quality paperback includes reader's discussion guide.

5½ x 8¼, 192 pp, Quality PB, 978-1-59473-106-8 **$14.99**

HC, 192 pp, 978-1-893361-72-0 **$19.95**

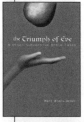

The Triumph of Eve & Other Subversive Bible Tales

by Matt Biers-Ariel

Many people were taught and remember only a one-dimensional Bible. These engaging retellings are the antidote to this—they're witty, often hilarious, always profound, and invite you to grapple with questions and issues that are often hidden in the original text.

5½ x 8¼, 192 pp, Quality PB, 978-1-59473-176-1 **$14.99**

Also avail.: **The Triumph of Eve Teacher's Guide**

8½ x 11, 44 pp, PB, 978-1-59473-152-5 **$8.99**

Wisdom in the Telling

Finding Inspiration and Grace in Traditional Folktales and Myths Retold

by Lorraine Hartin-Gelardi

6 x 9, 224 pp, HC, 978-1-59473-185-3 **$19.99**

Religious Etiquette / Reference

How to Be a Perfect Stranger, 4th Edition: The Essential Religious Etiquette Handbook Edited by Stuart M. Matlins and Arthur J. Magida

The indispensable guidebook to help the well-meaning guest when visiting other people's religious ceremonies. A straightforward guide to the rituals and celebrations of the major religions and denominations in the United States and Canada from the perspective of an interested guest of any other faith, based on information obtained from authorities of each religion. Belongs in every living room, library and office. Covers:

African American Methodist Churches • Assemblies of God • Bahá'í • Baptist • Buddhist • Christian Church (Disciples of Christ) • Christian Science (Church of Christ, Scientist) • Churches of Christ • Episcopalian and Anglican • Hindu • Islam • Jehovah's Witnesses • Jewish • Lutheran • Mennonite/Amish • Methodist • Mormon (Church of Jesus Christ of Latter-day Saints) • Native American/First Nations • Orthodox Churches • Pentecostal Church of God • Presbyterian • Quaker (Religious Society of Friends) • Reformed Church in America/Canada • Roman Catholic • Seventh-day Adventist • Sikh • Unitarian Universalist • United Church of Canada • United Church of Christ

6 x 9, 432 pp, Quality PB, 978-1-59473-140-2 **$19.99**

The Perfect Stranger's Guide to Funerals and Grieving Practices: A Guide to Etiquette in Other People's Religious Ceremonies Edited by Stuart M. Matlins

6 x 9, 240 pp, Quality PB, 978-1-893361-20-1 **$16.95**

The Perfect Stranger's Guide to Wedding Ceremonies: A Guide to Etiquette in Other People's Religious Ceremonies Edited by Stuart M. Matlins

6 x 9, 208 pp, Quality PB, 978-1-893361-19-5 **$16.95**

Spiritual Poetry—The Mystic Poets

Experience these mystic poets as you never have before. Each beautiful, compact book includes: a brief introduction to the poet's time and place; a summary of the major themes of the poet's mysticism and religious tradition; essential selections from the poet's most important works; and an appreciative preface by a contemporary spiritual writer.

Hafiz
The Mystic Poets
Preface by Ibrahim Gamard

Hafiz is known throughout the world as Persia's greatest poet, with sales of his poems in Iran today only surpassed by those of the Qur'an itself. His probing and joyful verse speaks to people from all backgrounds who long to taste and feel divine love and experience harmony with all living things.
5 x 7¼, 144 pp, HC, 978-1-59473-009-2 **$16.99**

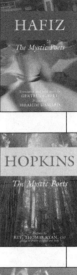

Hopkins
The Mystic Poets
Preface by Rev. Thomas Ryan, CSP

Gerard Manley Hopkins, Christian mystical poet, is beloved for his use of fresh language and startling metaphors to describe the world around him. Although his verse is lovely, beneath the surface lies a searching soul, wrestling with and yearning for God.
5 x 7¼, 112 pp, HC, 978-1-59473-010-8 **$16.99**

Tagore
The Mystic Poets
Preface by Swami Adiswarananda

Rabindranath Tagore is often considered the "Shakespeare" of modern India. A great mystic, Tagore was the teacher of W. B. Yeats and Robert Frost, the close friend of Albert Einstein and Mahatma Gandhi, and the winner of the Nobel Prize for Literature. This beautiful sampling of Tagore's two most important works, *The Gardener* and *Gitanjali*, offers a glimpse into his spiritual vision that has inspired people around the world.
5 x 7¼, 144 pp, HC, 978-1-59473-008-5 **$16.99**

Whitman
The Mystic Poets
Preface by Gary David Comstock

Walt Whitman was the most innovative and influential poet of the nineteenth century. This beautiful sampling of Whitman's most important poetry from *Leaves of Grass*, and selections from his prose writings, offers a glimpse into the spiritual side of his most radical themes—love for country, love for others, and love of Self.
5 x 7¼, 192 pp, HC, 978-1-59473-041-2 **$16.99**

Journeys of Simplicity
Traveling Light with Thomas Merton, Bashō, Edward Abbey, Annie Dillard & Others

Invites you to consider a more graceful way of traveling through life. Use the included journal pages (in PB only) to help you get started on your own spiritual journey.

Ed. by Philip Harnden
5 x 7¼, 144 pp, Quality PB, 978-1-59473-181-5 **$12.99**
128 pp, HC, 978-1-893361-76-8 **$16.95**

Spiritual Biography / Reference

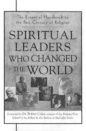

Spiritual Leaders Who Changed the World
The Essential Handbook to the Past Century of Religion
Edited by Ira Rifkin and the Editors at SkyLight Paths; Foreword by Dr. Robert Coles
An invaluable reference to the most important spiritual leaders of the past 100 years.
6 x 9, 304 pp, 15+ b/w photos, Quality PB, 978-1-59473-241-6 **$18.99**

Spiritual Biography—SkyLight Lives

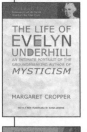

SkyLight Lives reintroduces the lives and works of key spiritual figures of our time—people who by their teaching or example have challenged our assumptions about spirituality and have caused us to look at it in new ways.

The Life of Evelyn Underhill
An Intimate Portrait of the Groundbreaking Author of Mysticism
by Margaret Cropper; Foreword by Dana Greene
Evelyn Underhill was a passionate writer and teacher who wrote elegantly on mysticism, worship, and devotional life.
6 x 9, 288 pp, 5 b/w photos, Quality PB, 978-1-893361-70-6 **$18.95**

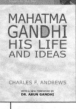

Mahatma Gandhi: His Life and Ideas
by Charles F. Andrews; Foreword by Dr. Arun Gandhi
Examines from a contemporary Christian activist's point of view the religious ideas and political dynamics that influenced the birth of the peaceful resistance movement.
6 x 9, 336 pp, 5 b/w photos, Quality PB, 978-1-893361-89-8 **$18.95**

Simone Weil: A Modern Pilgrimage
by Robert Coles
The extraordinary life of the spiritual philosopher who's been called both saint and madwoman.
6 x 9, 208 pp, Quality PB, 978-1-893361-34-8 **$16.95**

Zen Effects: The Life of Alan Watts
by Monica Furlong
Through his widely popular books and lectures, Alan Watts (1915–1973) did more to introduce Eastern philosophy and religion to Western minds than any figure before or since.
6 x 9, 264 pp, Quality PB, 978-1-893361-32-4 **$16.95**

More Spiritual Biography

Bede Griffiths: An Introduction to His Interspiritual Thought
by Wayne Teasdale
The first study of his contemplative experience and thought, exploring the intersection of Hinduism and Christianity.
6 x 9, 288 pp, Quality PB, 978-1-893361-77-5 **$18.95**

The Soul of the Story: Meetings with Remarkable People
by Rabbi David Zeller
Inspiring and entertaining, this compelling collection of spiritual adventures assures us that no spiritual lesson truly learned is ever lost.
6 x 9, 288 pp, HC, 978-1-58023-272-2 **$21.99** *(a Jewish Lights book)*

Sacred Texts—SkyLight Illuminations Series

Offers today's spiritual seeker an accessible entry into the great classic texts of the world's spiritual traditions. Each classic is presented in an accessible translation, with facing pages of guided commentary from experts, giving you the keys you need to understand the history, context and meaning of the text. This series enables you, whatever your background, to experience and understand classic spiritual texts directly, and to make them a part of your life.

CHRISTIANITY

The End of Days: Essential Selections from Apocalyptic Texts—Annotated & Explained *Annotation by Robert G. Clouse*
Helps you understand the complex Christian visions of the end of the world.
5½ x 8½, 224 pp, Quality PB, 978-1-59473-170-9 **$16.99**

The Hidden Gospel of Matthew: Annotated & Explained
Translation & Annotation by Ron Miller
Takes you deep into the text cherished around the world to discover the words and events that have the strongest connection to the historical Jesus.
5½ x 8½, 272 pp, Quality PB, 978-1-59473-038-2 **$16.99**

The Lost Sayings of Jesus: Teachings from Ancient Christian, Jewish, Gnostic and Islamic Sources—Annotated & Explained
Translation & Annotation by Andrew Phillip Smith; Foreword by Stephan A. Hoeller
This collection of more than three hundred sayings depicts Jesus as a Wisdom teacher who speaks to people of all faiths as a mystic and spiritual master.
5½ x 8½, 240 pp, Quality PB, 978-1-59473-172-3 **$16.99**

Philokalia: The Eastern Christian Spiritual Texts—Selections Annotated & Explained *Annotation by Allyne Smith; Translation by G. E. H. Palmer, Phillip Sherrard and Bishop Kallistos Ware*
The first approachable introduction to the wisdom of the Philokalia, which is the classic text of Eastern Christian spirituality.
5½ x 8½, 240 pp, Quality PB, 978-1-59473-103-7 **$16.99**

The Sacred Writings of Paul: Selections Annotated & Explained
Translation & Annotation by Ron Miller
Explores the apostle Paul's core message of spiritual equality, freedom and joy.
5½ x 8½, 224 pp, Quality PB, 978-1-59473-213-3 **$16.99**

Sex Texts from the Bible: Selections Annotated & Explained
Translation & Annotation by Teresa J. Hornsby; Foreword by Amy-Jill Levine
Offers surprising insight into our modern sexual lives.
5½ x 8½, 208 pp, Quality PB, 978-1-59473-217-1 **$16.99**

Spiritual Writings on Mary: Annotated & Explained
Annotation by Mary Ford-Grabowsky; Foreword by Andrew Harvey
Examines the role of Mary, the mother of Jesus, as a source of inspiration in history and in life today. 5½ x 8½, 288 pp, Quality PB, 978-1-59473-001-6 **$16.99**

The Way of a Pilgrim: The Jesus Prayer Journey—Annotated & Explained
Translation & Annotation by Gleb Pokrovsky; Foreword by Andrew Harvey
This classic of Russian spirituality is the delightful account of one man who sets out to learn the prayer of the heart, also known as the "Jesus prayer."
5½ x 8½, 160 pp, Illus., Quality PB, 978-1-893361-31-7 **$14.95**

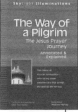

Sacred Texts—cont.

MORMONISM

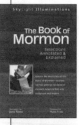

The Book of Mormon: Selections Annotated & Explained
Annotation by Jana Riess; Foreword by Phyllis Tickle
Explores the sacred epic that is cherished by more than twelve million members of the LDS church as the keystone of their faith.
5½ x 8½ , 272 pp, Quality PB, 978-1-59473-076-4 **$16.99**

NATIVE AMERICAN

Native American Stories of the Sacred: Annotated & Explained
Retold & Annotated by Evan T. Pritchard
Intended for more than entertainment, these teaching tales contain elegantly simple illustrations of time-honored truths.
5½ x 8½, 272 pp, Quality PB, 978-1-59473-112-9 **$16.99**

GNOSTICISM

Gnostic Writings on the Soul: Annotated & Explained
Translation & Annotation by Andrew Phillip Smith; Foreword by Stephan A. Hoeller
Reveals the inspiring ways your soul can remember and return to its unique, divine purpose.
5½ x 8½, 144 pp, Quality PB, 978-1-59473-220-1 **$16.99**

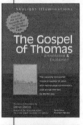

The Gospel of Philip: Annotated & Explained
Translation & Annotation by Andrew Phillip Smith; Foreword by Stevan Davies
Reveals otherwise unrecorded sayings of Jesus and fragments of Gnostic mythology.
5½ x 8½, 160 pp, Quality PB, 978-1-59473-111-2 **$16.99**

The Gospel of Thomas: Annotated & Explained
Translation & Annotation by Stevan Davies Sheds new light on the origins of Christianity and portrays Jesus as a wisdom-loving sage.
5½ x 8½, 192 pp, Quality PB, 978-1-893361-45-4 **$16.99**

The Secret Book of John: The Gnostic Gospel—Annotated & Explained
Translation & Annotation by Stevan Davies The most significant and influential text of the ancient Gnostic religion.
5½ x 8½, 208 pp, Quality PB, 978-1-59473-082-5 **$16.99**

JUDAISM

The Divine Feminine in Biblical Wisdom Literature
Selections Annotated & Explained
Translation & Annotation by Rabbi Rami Shapiro; Foreword by Rev. Cynthia Bourgeault, PhD
Uses the Hebrew books of Psalms, Proverbs, Song of Songs, Ecclesiastes and Job, Wisdom literature and the Wisdom of Solomon to clarify who Wisdom is.
5½ x 8½, 240 pp, Quality PB, 978-1-59473-109-9 **$16.99**

Ethics of the Sages: *Pirke Avot*—Annotated & Explained
Translation & Annotation by Rabbi Rami Shapiro Clarifies the ethical teachings of the early Rabbis. 5½ x 8½, 192 pp, Quality PB, 978-1-59473-207-2 **$16.99**

Hasidic Tales: Annotated & Explained
Translation & Annotation by Rabbi Rami Shapiro
Introduces the legendary tales of the impassioned Hasidic rabbis, presenting them as stories rather than as parables. 5½ x 8½, 240 pp, Quality PB, 978-1-893361-86-7 **$16.95**

The Hebrew Prophets: Selections Annotated & Explained
Translation & Annotation by Rabbi Rami Shapiro; Foreword by Zalman M. Schachter-Shalomi
Focuses on the central themes covered by all the Hebrew prophets.
5½ x 8½, 224 pp, Quality PB, 978-1-59473-037-5 **$16.99**

Zohar: Annotated & Explained *Translation & Annotation by Daniel C. Matt*
The best-selling author of *The Essential Kabbalah* brings together in one place the most important teachings of the Zohar, the canonical text of Jewish mystical tradition.
5½ x 8½, 176 pp, Quality PB, 978-1-893361-51-5 **$15.99**

Sacred Texts—cont.

ISLAM

The Qur'an and Sayings of Prophet Muhammad
Selections Annotated & Explained
Annotation by Sohaib N. Sultan; Translation by Yusuf Ali; Revised by Sohaib N. Sultan
Foreword by Jane I. Smith
Explores how the timeless wisdom of the Qur'an can enrich your own spiritual journey.
5½ x 8½, 256 pp, Quality PB, 978-1-59473-222-5 **$16.99**

Rumi and Islam: Selections from His Stories, Poems, and Discourses—Annotated & Explained
Translation & Annotation by Ibrahim Gamard
Focuses on Rumi's place within the Sufi tradition of Islam, providing insight into the mystical side of the religion.
5½ x 8½, 240 pp, Quality PB, 978-1-59473-002-3 **$15.99**

EASTERN RELIGIONS

The Art of War—Spirituality for Conflict
Annotated & Explained
by Sun Tzu; Annotation by Thomas Huynh; Translation by Thomas Huynh and the Editors at Sonshi.com; Foreword by Thomas Cleary; Preface by Marc Benioff
Highlights principles that encourage a perceptive and spiritual approach to conflict.
5½ x 8½, 192 pp (est), Quality PB, 978-1-59473-244-7 **$16.99**

Bhagavad Gita: Annotated & Explained
Translation by Shri Purohit Swami; Annotation by Kendra Crossen Burroughs
Explains references and philosophical terms, shares the interpretations of famous spiritual leaders and scholars, and more.
5½ x 8½, 192 pp, Quality PB, 978-1-893361-28-7 **$16.95**

Dhammapada: Annotated & Explained
Translation by Max Müller and revised by Jack Maguire; Annotation by Jack Maguire
Contains all of Buddhism's key teachings.
5½ x 8½, 160 pp, b/w photos, Quality PB, 978-1-893361-42-3 **$14.95**

Selections from the Gospel of Sri Ramakrishna
Annotated & Explained
Translation by Swami Nikhilananda; Annotation by Kendra Crossen Burroughs
Introduces the fascinating world of the Indian mystic and the universal appeal of his message.
5½ x 8½, 240 pp, b/w photos, Quality PB, 978-1-893361-46-1 **$16.95**

Tao Te Ching: Annotated & Explained
Translation & Annotation by Derek Lin; Foreword by Lama Surya Das
Introduces an Eastern classic in an accessible, poetic and completely original way.
5½ x 8½, 192 pp, Quality PB, 978-1-59473-204-1 **$16.99**

STOICISM

The Meditations of Marcus Aurelius
Selections Annotated & Explained
Annotation by Russell McNeil, PhD; Translation by George Long; Revised by Russell McNeil, PhD
Offers insightful and engaging commentary into the historical background of Stoicism.
5½ x 8½, 288 pp, Quality PB, 978-1-59473-236-2 **$16.99**

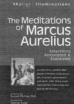

Spiritual Practice

Soul Fire: Accessing Your Creativity *by Rev. Thomas Ryan, CSP*
Shows you how to cultivate your creative spirit as a way to encourage personal growth.
6 x 9, 160 pp, Quality PB, 978-1-59473-243-0 **$16.99**

Running—The Sacred Art: Preparing to Practice
by Dr. Warren A. Kay; Foreword by Kristin Armstrong
Examines how your daily run can enrich your spiritual life.
5½ x 8½, 160 pp, Quality PB, 978-1-59473-227-0 **$16.99**

Hospitality—The Sacred Art: Discovering the Hidden Spiritual Power
of Invitation and Welcome *by Rev. Nanette Sawyer; Foreword by Rev. Dirk Ficca*
Explores how this ancient spiritual practice can transform your relationships.
5½ x 8½, 192 pp, Quality PB, 978-1-59473-228-7 **$16.99**

Thanking & Blessing—The Sacred Art: Spiritual Vitality through
Gratefulness *by Jay Marshall, PhD; Foreword by Philip Gulley*
Offers practical tips for uncovering the blessed wonder in our lives—even in try-
ing circumstances. 5½ x 8½, 176 pp, Quality PB, 978-1-59473-231-7 **$16.99**

Everyday Herbs in Spiritual Life: A Guide to Many Practices
by Michael J. Caduto; Foreword by Rosemary Gladstar Explores the power of herbs.
7 x 9, 208 pp, 21 b/w illustrations, Quality PB, 978-1-59473-174-7 **$16.99**

Divining the Body: Reclaim the Holiness of Your Physical Self *by Jan Phillips*
8 x 8, 256 pp, Quality PB, 978-1-59473-080-1 **$16.99**

Finding Time for the Timeless: Spirituality in the Workweek
by John McQuiston II Simple stories show you how refocus your daily life.
5½ x 6¾, 208 pp, HC, 978-1-59473-035-1 **$17.99**

The Gospel of Thomas: A Guidebook for Spiritual Practice
by Ron Miller; Translations by Stevan Davies
6 x 9, 160 pp, Quality PB, 978-1-59473-047-4 **$14.99**

Earth, Water, Fire, and Air: Essential Ways of Connecting to Spirit
by Cait Johnson 6 x 9, 224 pp, HC, 978-1-893361-65-2 **$19.95**

Labyrinths from the Outside In: Walking to Spiritual Insight—A Beginner's Guide
by Donna Schaper and Carole Ann Camp
6 x 9, 208 pp, b/w illus. and photos, Quality PB, 978-1-893361-18-8 **$16.95**

Practicing the Sacred Art of Listening: A Guide to Enrich Your Relationships
and Kindle Your Spiritual Life—The Listening Center Workshop
by Kay Lindahl 8 x 8, 176 pp, Quality PB, 978-1-893361-85-0 **$16.95**

Releasing the Creative Spirit: Unleash the Creativity in Your Life
by Dan Wakefield 7 x 10, 256 pp, Quality PB, 978-1-893361-36-2 **$16.95**

The Sacred Art of Bowing: Preparing to Practice
by Andi Young 5½ x 8½, 128 pp, b/w illus., Quality PB, 978-1-893361-82-9 **$14.95**

The Sacred Art of Chant: Preparing to Practice
by Ana Hernández 5½ x 8½, 192 pp, Quality PB, 978-1-59473-036-8 **$15.99**

The Sacred Art of Fasting: Preparing to Practice
by Thomas Ryan, CSP 5½ x 8½, 192 pp, Quality PB, 978-1-59473-078-8 **$15.99**

The Sacred Art of Forgiveness: Forgiving Ourselves and Others through God's Grace
by Marcia Ford 8 x 8, 176 pp, Quality PB, 978-1-59473-175-4 **$16.99**

The Sacred Art of Listening: Forty Reflections for Cultivating a Spiritual Practice
by Kay Lindahl; Illustrations by Amy Schnapper
8 x 8, 160 pp, b/w illus., Quality PB, 978-1-893361-44-7 **$16.99**

The Sacred Art of Lovingkindness: Preparing to Practice
by Rabbi Rami Shapiro; Foreword by Marcia Ford 5½ x 8½, 176 pp, Quality PB, 978-1-59473-151-8 **$16.99**

Sacred Speech: A Practical Guide for Keeping Spirit in Your Speech
by Rev. Donna Schaper 6 x 9, 176 pp, Quality PB, 978-1-59473-068-9 **$15.99**
HC, 978-1-893361-74-4 **$21.95**

Spirituality of the Seasons

Autumn: A Spiritual Biography of the Season
Edited by Gary Schmidt and Susan M. Felch; Illustrations by Mary Azarian
Rejoice in autumn as a time of preparation and reflection. Includes Wendell Berry, David James Duncan, Robert Frost, A. Bartlett Giamatti, E. B. White, P. D. James, Julian of Norwich, Garret Keizer, Tracy Kidder, Anne Lamott, May Sarton.
6 x 9, 320 pp, 5 b/w illus., Quality PB, 978-1-59473-118-1 **$18.99**

Spring: A Spiritual Biography of the Season
Edited by Gary Schmidt and Susan M. Felch; Illustrations by Mary Azarian
Explore the gentle unfurling of spring and reflect on how nature celebrates rebirth and renewal. Includes Jane Kenyon, Lucy Larcom, Harry Thurston, Nathaniel Hawthorne, Noel Perrin, Annie Dillard, Martha Ballard, Barbara Kingsolver, Dorothy Wordsworth, Donald Hall, David Brill, Lionel Basney, Isak Dinesen, Paul Laurence Dunbar. 6 x 9, 352 pp, 6 b/w illus., Quality PB, 978-1-59473-246-1 **$18.99**

Summer: A Spiritual Biography of the Season
Edited by Gary Schmidt and Susan M. Felch; Illustrations by Barry Moser
"A sumptuous banquet…. These selections lift up an exquisite wholeness found within an everyday sophistication." — ★ *Publishers Weekly* starred review
Includes Anne Lamott, Luci Shaw, Ray Bradbury, Richard Selzer, Thomas Lynch, Walt Whitman, Carl Sandburg, Sherman Alexie, Madeleine L'Engle, Jamaica Kincaid.
6 x 9, 304 pp, 5 b/w illus., Quality PB, 978-1-59473-183-9 **$18.99**
HC, 978-1-59473-083-2 **$21.99**

Winter: A Spiritual Biography of the Season
Edited by Gary Schmidt and Susan M. Felch; Illustrations by Barry Moser
"This outstanding anthology features top-flight nature and spirituality writers on the fierce, inexorable season of winter…. Remarkably lively and warm, despite the icy subject." — ★ *Publishers Weekly* starred review
Includes Will Campbell, Rachel Carson, Annie Dillard, Donald Hall, Ron Hansen, Jane Kenyon, Jamaica Kincaid, Barry Lopez, Kathleen Norris, John Updike, E. B. White.
6 x 9, 288 pp, 6 b/w illus., Deluxe PB w/flaps, 978-1-893361-92-8 **$18.95**
HC, 978-1-893361-53-9 **$21.95**

Spirituality / Animal Companions

Blessing the Animals: Prayers and Ceremonies to Celebrate God's Creatures, Wild and Tame *Edited by Lynn L. Caruso* 5 x 7¼, 256 pp, HC, 978-1-59473-145-7 **$19.99**

Remembering My Pet: A Kid's Own Spiritual Workbook for When a Pet Dies
by Nechama Liss-Levinson, PhD, and Rev. Molly Phinney Baskette, MDiv; Foreword by Lynn L. Caruso
8 x 10, 48 pp, 2-color text, HC, 978-1-59473-221-3 **$16.99**

What Animals Can Teach Us about Spirituality: Inspiring Lessons from Wild and Tame Creatures *by Diana L. Guerrero* 6 x 9, 176 pp, Quality PB, 978-1-893361-84-3 **$16.95**

Spirituality—A Week Inside

Come and Sit: A Week Inside Meditation Centers
by Marcia Z. Nelson; Foreword by Wayne Teasdale
6 x 9, 224 pp, b/w photos, Quality PB, 978-1-893361-35-5 **$16.95**

Lighting the Lamp of Wisdom: A Week Inside a Yoga Ashram
by John Ittner; Foreword by Dr. David Frawley
6 x 9, 192 pp, 10+ b/w photos, Quality PB, 978-1-893361-52-2 **$15.95**

Making a Heart for God: A Week Inside a Catholic Monastery
by Dianne Aprile; Foreword by Brother Patrick Hart, OCSO
6 x 9, 224 pp, b/w photos, Quality PB, 978-1-893361-49-2 **$16.95**

Waking Up: A Week Inside a Zen Monastery
by Jack Maguire; Foreword by John Daido Loori, Roshi
6 x 9, 224 pp, b/w photos, Quality PB, 978-1-893361-55-3 **$16.95**; HC, 978-1-893361-13-3 **$21.95**

About SKYLIGHT PATHS Publishing

SkyLight Paths Publishing is creating a place where people of different spiritual traditions come together for challenge and inspiration, a place where we can help each other understand the mystery that lies at the heart of our existence.

Through spirituality, our religious beliefs are increasingly becoming a part of our lives—rather than *apart* from our lives. While many of us may be more interested than ever in spiritual growth, we may be less firmly planted in traditional religion. Yet, we do want to deepen our relationship to the sacred, to learn from our own as well as from other faith traditions, and to practice in new ways.

SkyLight Paths sees both believers and seekers as a community that increasingly transcends traditional boundaries of religion and denomination—people wanting to learn from each other, *walking together, finding the way.*

For your information and convenience, at the back of this book we have provided a list of other SkyLight Paths books you might find interesting and useful. They cover the following subjects:

Buddhism / Zen	Global Spiritual	Monasticism
Catholicism	Perspectives	Mysticism
Children's Books	Gnosticism	Poetry
Christianity	Hinduism /	Prayer
Comparative	Vedanta	Religious Etiquette
Religion	Inspiration	Retirement
Current Events	Islam / Sufism	Spiritual Biography
Earth-Based	Judaism	Spiritual Direction
Spirituality	Kabbalah	Spirituality
Enneagram	Meditation	Women's Interest
	Midrash Fiction	Worship

Or phone, fax, mail or e-mail to: SKYLIGHT PATHS Publishing
Sunset Farm Offices, Route 4 • P.O. Box 237 • Woodstock, Vermont 05091
Tel: (802) 457-4000 • Fax: (802) 457-4004 • www.skylightpaths.com
Credit card orders: (800) 962-4544 (8:30AM–5:30PM ET Monday–Friday)
Generous discounts on quantity orders. SATISFACTION GUARANTEED. Prices subject to change.